From SHOWING OFF *to* SHOWING UP

An Impostor's Journey
from Perfect to Present

NANCY REGAN

NIMBUS
PUBLISHING
— NIMBUS.CA —

Nimbus Publishing Limited
3660 Strawberry Hill Street, Halifax, NS, B3K 5A9
(902) 455-4286 nimbus.ca

Printed and bound in Canada

Editor: Whitney Moran
Design: John van der Woude
Cover photography: Timothy Richard
NB1577

Library and Archives Canada Cataloguing in Publication

Title: From showing off to showing up : an imposter's journey from perfect
    to present / Nancy Regan.
Names: Regan, Nancy (Television news anchor), author.
Identifiers: Canadiana (print) 20210379065 | Canadiana (ebook) 20210379162
    | ISBN 9781774710319 (softcover) | ISBN 9781774710647 (EPUB)
Subjects: LCSH: Regan, Nancy (Television news anchor) | LCSH: Women
    television news anchors—Canada—Biography. | LCSH: Television news
    anchors—Canada—Biography. | LCSH: Women television personalities—
    Canada—Biography. | LCSH: Television personalities—Canada—
    Biography. | LCSH: Public speaking. | LCSH: Self-confidence. | LCGFT:
    Autobiographies.
Classification: LCC PN4913.R44 A3 2022 | DDC 070.92—dc23

Nimbus Publishing acknowledges the financial support for its publishing activities from the Government of Canada, the Canada Council for the Arts, and from the Province of Nova Scotia. We are pleased to work in partnership with the Province of Nova Scotia to develop and promote our creative industries for the benefit of all Nova Scotians.

CONTENTS

MY PRACTICE: DOORWAYS TO PRESENCE

TO BE CONTINUED 255

INTRODUCTION

*"Out beyond ideas of wrongdoing and rightdoing,
there is a field. I'll meet you there.
When the soul lies down in that grass,
the world is too full to talk about.
Ideas, language, even the phrase 'each other'
doesn't make any sense."*

—Rumi

You may hate this book.

Don't you just love language?! One of my favourite things about words is their ability to hold different meanings, even when grouped in the exact same way. That first sentence of mine—which might strike you as a strange way to launch a book—can be perceived as possibility or permission. Here's my explanation: yes and yes. The *possibility* exists that the content and intent of this book will not appeal to you. While it may resonate profoundly for some, it may drop with a thud at your feet. That's okay. It's not for you. And here's the *permission* part. I give you my blessing to dislike it. To be honest, it's the *possibility* of your disdain that gives this book wings.

You see, most of my life has been devoted to collecting gold stars. Approval has been my most severe addiction. But like any drug or substance, as it turns out, approval cannot fill me up. Well, that's not entirely true. It can make my heart sing—for a moment. But after the singing, the sinking. Despite living a privileged life and having many opportunities that led to a fascinating career, I still fell victim to deep-seated feelings of inadequacy. I stood for years in a spotlight, yet it never really lit me up. It couldn't. Like any high, it was always short-lived, and the aftermath brought truth into focus. That's what this book is about for me: bringing my truth into focus. First and foremost, for me. But I also believe that in telling our stories, we free others. With this book, I'm embracing all parts of me, in the hope it will help you accept all parts of *you*. Because frankly, I believe that's the only true path to comfort—to serenity.

I'm asking you to join me on a journey that might seem a bit like something out of an adventure movie. We're going to venture into a deep, dark pit that seems impossible to scramble out of— complete with steep walls, and maybe even some triggered booby traps à la *Indiana Jones*. My own Temple of Doom. The good news is, I lived to tell the tale. At times, the very writing of this book dragged me back into that darkness, but it also brought me to a whole new understanding—that it's an adventure I can *choose*. Now I've got all sorts of tools to help me find my way out and get back to living my life. That's my personal version of the Holy Grail, and it's what I'm going to endeavour to share.

As the longtime co-host of a TV newsmagazine, I interviewed some of the biggest stars in the world (Oprah, Madonna, Russell Crowe, Meg Ryan, Mel Gibson...) and spent thousands of hours on live TV, but what you might never have guessed—what I never wanted anyone to know—is that behind my seemingly confident exterior was an interior landscape littered with perfectionism, insecurity, and a paralyzing fear of failure. It's something I have struggled with for my entire life, but working toward overcoming those challenges enriches my life, and now it fuels my ability to help others.

Having spent most of my life on one stage or another, as a TV broadcaster, actor, and speaker, these days I'm a presentation coach. Those three aspects of my career have woven themselves together to support me in coaching others in the art of presentation. I love helping clients dig into whatever is holding them back, and in my experience, the words *public* and *speaking*, when combined, strike terror into most people's hearts.

Jerry Seinfeld captured it best when he zeroed in on the humour beneath the popular statistic that public speaking is people's number-one fear. As he so eloquently quipped, this means that at a funeral, most people would rather be lying in the casket than giving the eulogy. This is hilariously close to the truth. So the question is, what are we so afraid of?

The book you hold in your hands was originally meant to be a guide to overcoming the fear of public speaking, which is the work I do one-on-one with clients. Not long into the collaborative process with my editor, though, she told me she thought focusing solely on public speaking was limiting the book's potential, that the structure was strangling what was morphing into a more organic project. In my mind it was always meant to be a subversively soulful approach to helping people learn to stand comfortably in the spotlight—that's what I love doing—but my editor recognized that I was hiding part of myself behind the podium. And so, this book is less about doing and more about *being*. I'm stepping out of the spiritual closet and I'm hoping you'll come along.

Although the content of this book isn't specifically focused on the fear of public speaking, I do think this common phobia provides a valid and valuable example, and it's the realm from which I draw a lot of my own experience to share with you. What I've realized through my journey is that my discomfort with being myself in the spotlight, boiled down, was plain, old-fashioned, primitive fear. My craving to be accepted was just the flip side of my deep dread of rejection.

When coaching, I always lead with the firm conviction that public speaking is just like shooting a foul shot in basketball; it's a skill that can be acquired, practiced, and mastered. However, if you really want to be comfortable in the spotlight, you've got to get comfortable with yourself. For most of us, there's a deeper issue that lies beneath the fear of public speaking: the fear of public *being*. And beneath that, profound self-limiting beliefs that we are not smart enough, not capable enough, not likable enough... just not enough. Let me be clear, though, I'm not writing about *us*; I'm writing about me, vulnerably and honestly, in the hope that you might see something of yourself in my experiences, and begin (or continue) your own journey.

I have thought a lot about why some people have such a negative reaction to the words "self-help," and it all seems to lead back to the ego. Strength is celebrated in our world, while weakness is given a wide berth. This basic equation has long fed the stigma around therapy. For this reason, self-help books often get a bad rap. But here's the irony: true strength requires vulnerability.

Without being able to understand and accept my weakness, my strength was just a facade. When I finally began to recognize this, I starting reading...a lot, and I have found many self-help books immensely helpful on my own path. Maybe I've been lucky that the right ones always seemed to land in my lap at the right time, but I also believe these books are meant to be tools. A hammer won't do the work for you unless you do your part. Neither will a book aimed at helping you expand your sense of self. If you don't do the prescribed "work," you won't get results. That's where practice comes in.

In these pages, I'll share stories from my career and personal life that demonstrate my close relationship to fear. (In fact, you could say fear and I grew up together.) But I'm not coming from a been-there-done-that smugness. I'm standing neck-deep in vulnerability, willing and eager to help you understand the journey that brought me from fake to fabulous. Whoa!—cue the screeching-stop sound FX—did I really just describe myself as fabulous?! Yes, I did, and it's my mission to help you find your fabulousness too. Find it, embrace it, love it, shine it! 'Cause you're not doing yourself or anyone else any favours by playing small.

As if I wasn't already being vulnerable enough, I've made the choice to share my personal poems in this book. Poetry helps me make sense of the world. I love the way it can bring complex issues into sharp focus—often with few words. Writing poems is a form of therapy for me, and they seem to flow through me rather than from me. What I've discovered, to my great surprise, is that when these simple little poems of mine are birthed in a state of pure honesty, they tend to resonate with others as well. I offer them up with humility and love.

Stop playing small
Stop passing the ball
It's time to square up & shoot

Stop being precious
Stop being gracious
It's time to hit UNMUTE

You've always been quiet
You've always been good
Trying to stay in your BOX

But that's not what you came for
You're called now to be MORE
And the first step's controlling your thoughts

Say this: "I am LARGE"
Repeat: "I am READY
To take up more space in the world

Shining some LIGHT
For those still in fright
Flying my flag UNFURLED"

My belief is that you can't live *large* until you've made peace with the past. Until you make sense of your suffering, it will continue. I'm digging into my own pit of fear to help light the pathway out of that suffering, and to demonstrate how old wounds can keep us imprisoned in the present. But here's my disclaimer: Chances are you've had it worse than I have. Alcoholism. Abuse.

Neglect. Violence. Racism. Bullying. Belittling. These are some of the brutal realities you might have grown up with. The unfairness of childhood as a battleground takes my breath away. But as I exhale, releasing my thoughts and memories onto these pages, I want to bring clarity to the reason I feel my story might be helpful—even if the obstacles I have overcome seem minuscule in relation to the landscape of your life. In fact, I believe it is *because* my own stones might seem inconsequential in relation to the boulders you'll find in your own dig, that it is useful. If I bear scars from struggles that may seem negligible to you (the phrases "white privilege" and "First World problems" spring to mind), then it should come as no surprise that you bear scars too. Many of them deeper, more raw, and soothed only with the help and support of others.

Who are you to write about this? That's the whisper of my inner critic—the same voice that says, *Who are you to shine? Who are you to speak out? Who are you to take up space?* As much as I've allowed this voice free rein over the years, I finally understand that I can't negate my own experience by comparing it to others'. My wounds are my wounds, and ignoring and belittling them does nothing to heal them.

I've discovered many forms of healing in my journey, but the most powerful by far is presence. You could say it's my secret weapon.

SHOWING OFF VERSUS SHOWING UP

At the end of the book, I'll share some of my own Doorways to Presence—my personal practices for extricating myself from the past and future and planting me back in the present moment—how learning the art of presence, or *being in the moment*, helped me step out of social anxiety and fear. Onstage, a significant part of that transformation comes through shifting a speaker's focus from *performance* to *contribution,* but this is equally true offstage, in our daily lives. In my terminology, Showing Off means "presenting" yourself to others with a focus on *their* judgement. Showing UP, in contrast, is bringing your authentic self to the interaction—that is, without the internal dialogue that can so easily undermine your message, your power, and your presence.

When I talk about Showing Off, I'm describing our propensity as humans for adopting a character just as actors take on roles. Developing it and filling it out to create just the right impression in the minds of others. Showing UP, on the other hand, is what happens when we arrive on this planet. Here I am. Unadulterated. Un-*adult*-erated. Showing Off is what we learn to do in order to fit in, win approval, and often protect ourselves. We learn to present *our selves* according to the expectations and judgements of others. I learned early to mould myself into whatever form might earn the most praise. Here's the kicker: Showing Off is driven by our hunger for acceptance and belonging, but I believe the only way to really earn those treasures is through a commitment to Showing UP.

I've come to understand that the path to true comfort in any spotlight is simply the path to comfort in my own skin, in my own life. But to learn that, I had to get *uncomfortable.*

————————————

Just be yourself.

I don't have any data to back up this claim, but I'm pretty sure this is the most oft-quoted advice regarding the fear of stepping into the spotlight, going for a job interview, or heading out on a first date. I know I was presented with this little gem when I was a teenager, and I've heard it countless times since in many different contexts. But I have a theory that blows it out of the water. Let's start with the innocuous sounding "just" in this statement. This is the first fatal flaw. "Just" suggests simplicity, and for many of us, being ourselves in front of others is not a simple task—in fact, everything in my experience has taught me that it can be one of the most difficult. "Be" is no less problematic, but we'll get to that later. Right now, we're going to zero in on "Yourself."

In order to be *yourself*, you need to fundamentally understand who you are. In my experience, part of really getting to know yourself involves figuring out what it is that you *don't like* about yourself. And what has caused those disturbances to your ego's ecosystem? Your *egosystem*, let's say. The next step is coming to terms with those parts of you that don't fit comfortably. In order to raise your self-esteem, you've got to improve your self-acceptance. Ideally, you'll eventually come to understand you *are* enough, and learn to like yourself. That might be the end of the story. But it can get even better, when you realize you're *more* than enough and completely worthy of love—your own and others'.

This is the adventure I hinted at before. It's admittedly challenging, but it might be the most rewarding expedition on which you'll ever embark. It has been for me, and I'm eager to share with you. But please understand my motivation. I'm taking you along on this very personal journey so that you might discover a path that will serve your own growth as my journey has served mine. It's a trip from *fear* to *love*, and while it's a lot of ground to cover, it's also as simple as shifting gears. And for the record, this journey of mine is far from over. The more I learn, the more I learn how much I have to learn. Consider the Socratic Paradox: "The more I know, the more I realize I know nothing." And now let's modify it a little bit. Tell yourself, as I often do: "I am a work in progress—a work in practice." This is something I am grateful to have accepted in my own life. It's a long way from the perfectionism that constricted me for decades, and it's an infinitely more expansive way to live.

I still believe that anyone looking to be a better speaker will benefit from reading this book, but now that I'm really Showing UP, I know it's about so much more. If you work on being a better human—and by that, I mean a fuller expression of yourself and your humanity—you'll open up a life with more connection, more meaning, and more joy.

MY JOURNEY
Getting Present
with the Past

HOLE

"*Maybe you are searching among the branches
for what only appears at the roots.*"

—Rumi

Remember how much fun it was as a kid to climb up on a swing and get a push? The rush of air through your hair, the exhilaration of the perfect dose of fear to awaken all your senses. As we got comfortable, our parents would push us a little harder, allowing us to feel a fuller spectrum of that swinging sensation. It set us free, and for most of us it was our first experience of flight. Eventually, we graduated to the underduck—you know, when the "pusher" would run with and then under the swing, unleashing pure glee for the swinger? But of course, adventure and risk are fast friends, and injury could ensue from this otherwise delightful endeavour. If you weren't holding on tightly, you could fall off. Cuts, scrapes, and bruises would usually be the worst of it, but part of the escapade was defying the fear and embracing the fun.

Isn't this how we should all live our lives—open to adventure, embracing a healthy dose of *fear*? But we tend to grow out of this. I know I did.

As a kid, I loved the Zipper—at the time, the most daring ride at the fair. After navigating a long lineup, we eagerly climbed into an oval cage, got strapped in, and the door was latched. Then, the large wheel on which the cages were mounted started to turn— but our compartment turned too, for it was attached only by an axle. The next few minutes were a thrilling blur of fear and fun. When the ride was over we stumbled off, happy to be on *terra firma* once again but also laughing our heads off, adrenaline still surging through us.

In my experience, growing up teaches us that fear is to be avoided at all costs; that what we need, above all else, is control.

Fast-forward to motherhood. When my boys were six and eight years old, I found myself on a Ferris wheel with them. Pretty tame, right? Not so, as it turned out. As you likely know, the nature of this ride is that before and after the wheel turns unimpeded, it must methodically stop and start, allowing the exit and entrance of passengers. These little stops are part of the "fun"—you're left hanging, waiting for the motion to resume. But that day, some kind of problem stopped the wheel for ten eternal minutes while we were at the very top of the rotation. It was windy and we were rocking, and while my kids were exhilarated, I was experiencing something very different. Here I was with my two sweet boys, and my primary life's work as their mother was to protect them. It may have only been the Ferris wheel, but with every gust of wind, I felt the tumultuous terror of the Zipper—only without the fun. It wasn't rational; it was pure instinct. And every cell in my body was revolting against this lack of control.

Rock-a-bye Baby,
On the treetop,
When the wind blows,
The cradle will rock.
When the bough breaks,
The cradle will fall.
Down will come Baby,
Cradle and all.

What if the bough breaks? What if our "seat" gets loosened by the wind? What if the maintenance has been shoddy? What if one of my active boys squirms away from me and falls? What if we all fall? What if we die? This torturous spiral of thoughts is exactly the kind of mental tornado that happens for so many of us when we are stepping into the spotlight. Feeling like we might die. *What if the bough breaks? What if I screw up? What if I forget my material? What if they don't like me? What if they think I'm stupid? What if they know I'm stupid?* My job in this book is to strengthen not only your bough, but your whole damn tree. Helping you grow roots that will allow you to bend in the wind without breaking.

If you look around your world, and likely even in the mirror, you'll see a vast number of people who are like brittle branches. Desperate for others to see them as sufficient, while secretly afraid they're not enough. Terrified for the world to find them out, they use control as a crutch, trying to prevent disaster. Been there, done that.

In 2019, I was involved with a production company that put together an event featuring internationally bestselling writer Elizabeth Gilbert, of *Eat, Pray, Love* fame. I'd interviewed her on my podcast *The Soul Booth* a few months earlier, and that conversation was life-changing for me (I'll tell you why later). But something she said onstage during that gathering applies directly to this quest to uncover our fears.

Liz started by addressing the room, telling us all that she was on a mission. She had travelled all over the world and noticed that women everywhere seemed to have one thing in common. That if we could change this *one* thing, we could change our lives and change the world. That it was her personal goal to help create this enormous shift by convincing women to learn to do this one thing. Are you sitting on the edge of your seat? We were. She had employed all of her best storytelling techniques to tease us along, and then eventually she said, with great emphasis, "So what is this one thing I need to convince women everywhere to do?" And after a dramatic pause, she followed up with her simple answer in a calm and steady voice:

"Relax."

The entire audience burst into self-conscious laughter, the kind of wry chuckle that surfaces when you recognize an embarrassing truth about yourself. Liz then turned our attention to something else we had in common: our brains. In particular, she focused in on what's known as our *reptilian brain*: the oldest and most primitive part of this complex organ. This concept is based on a theory developed in the 1960s by American neuroscientist Paul MacLean. It should be noted that as a scientific model, it's since been debunked, but for the purposes of self-reflection and development, it's powerful. As the theory goes, our reptilian brain is concerned only with our most primal needs, widely referred to as the four Fs: fighting, fleeing, feeding, and, for the purposes of keeping it PG, let's just say procreating. But here's the brilliant assignment Liz Gilbert gave us. After describing how this part of our brain is the home of our fear, she encouraged us to get creative and personify it. Her suggestion: a big oaf of a cousin (maybe his name is Joey?) who is completely lacking in sophistication, but utterly and devotedly intent on protecting you, and as such, is deserving of compassion.

Actually, come to think of it, I'd like to call a time out! I want you to stop reading right now and do this exercise. Don't just take my word for the effectiveness of it. I want you to take a moment and give your own fear a name, and maybe even a personality. Heck, create a backstory if you feel like it. Just so you know I'm all in, here's mine: his name is GUS the Gator. He is the reptilian representation of my fear, doubt, and insecurity, and this book is all about my ongoing attempts to tame him. He's still a wild animal though, so it's a work in progress. For the record, GUS stands for "Give Up, Stupid," his favourite sweet nothing to whisper in my ear.

Okay, back to work. I'm going to ask you to do exactly what Liz Gilbert asked of us in the audience that day: write a letter to yourself—from your fear. I'll admit that at the time, I thought it was a ridiculous request. I remember sitting there, thinking, *Okay, Liz...I was with you every step of the way till now, but this is silly. This is not going to work!* I understood the concept. I've done enough free-writing to know that when I get still and silent and put a pen to paper, surprising things can be revealed. But this? No way. I figured I'd have to fake it. But guess what? It worked. And I promise you that if you do it right now, I'll share mine with you. A little later.

For the sake of illustration, let's go back to the fear of public speaking for a moment. In evolutionary terms, this particular fear seems sensible. I think about an old Dr. Seuss book I used to love as a child called *I Had Trouble in Getting to Solla Sollew*. In this book, a little creature becomes exasperated by his problems at home and sets off looking for greener pastures. Along the way he encounters a charismatic fellow who convinces him to come along in search of a beautiful city called Solla Sollew, "where they never have troubles, at least very few." After a series of harrowing adventures, they arrive in the legendary place only to find the city is not what it's cracked up to be, and the hero of the story returns home equipped to deal with the problems that dwell there. He's learned along his journey that he's more resourceful and stronger than he ever knew.

Now, you might suspect I'm telling you this story because I hope that's exactly how you'll feel at the end of this book. And I do. But that's not why I brought it up. I actually want to tell you about a specific illustration of a perilous moment in a place called Pompelmoose Pass. Our little hero suddenly finds himself surrounded by a whole lot of Poozers—devilish-looking, cat-like creatures that seem to be sizing him up for a feast. He's standing there by himself with all these eyes trained on him, knowing his life is in danger. This is my enduring visual image of the fear of public speaking. No wonder standing in a spotlight is fear-inducing. You may be onstage in front of an audience of highly evolved and educated people, but judging by the physiological response most of us experience, you might as well be a neanderthal facing a pack of sabre-toothed tigers.

This takes us back to those four Fs—the priorities of the reptilian brain. In this case, it's the three Fs: fight, flight, or freeze.

That is the urgent question our body attempts to answer when provoked by any sense of danger—even if we're not actually in physical danger. Maybe we're standing at a microphone, sitting in the hotseat on a Zoom call, or walking into a cocktail party full of strangers. I've felt it in many situations, even dressed in a ballgown in a luxurious hotel, about to accept an award for my own achievement! It's *social* fear, and it's deeply rooted in our concern about how others will perceive, and receive, us. But here's the interesting part: as far as our bodies are concerned, this fear of others' judgement masquerades as a physical threat to our very existence. So, what happens? Our heart rate quickens, our breath gets shallow, our muscles tense up, and we perspire. The bottom line is this: fear convinces us, at a basic physiological level, that we are in trouble, and our bodies start doing all the things they need to do to prepare to engage in battle—or beat a hasty retreat.

This is clearly not an optimal state to be in when standing in any kind of spotlight. However, if you've experienced this, you should take a lot of comfort in knowing that you are not alone. In fact, you're in excellent company. And no, I'm not just talking about me. Try Sir Laurence Olivier for size. Yes, at a time when he had already been broadly acknowledged as one of—if not the—best actors in the world, Sir Larry developed a brutal case of stage fright. In a fascinating 2013 article in the *Guardian*, director Michael Blakemore described how, during a production of *Long Day's Journey into Night*, the renowned performer "suddenly buckled under the weight of expectation that this reputation had placed on him." Olivier himself wrote in his autobiography about his stage fright, and the disconcerting light-headed experience of the audience "beginning to go giddily round."

I've certainly been confronted with that powerless feeling—most of us have, and it can be nauseating. But when it happens to us, we don't think about the fact that it's common. Instead, it's an excruciatingly singular and isolating event, and we maintain that sense of isolation by pretending it doesn't exist. So, here's where we climb back down off the stage, because that spotlight I'm talking about doesn't just exist there. Instead of stage fright, let's call it *life fright*.

There are a myriad of celebrities today who have admitted to struggling with anxiety, including some of the most successful people on the planet. Lady Gaga springs immediately to mind because of her public crusade to erase the stigma around mental illness. In a 2015 *Billboard* magazine article she said, "I've suffered through depression and anxiety my entire life. I still suffer with it every single day." Prince Harry and Oprah both opened up about their struggles in their television series, *The Me You Can't See*, a companion project to Oprah's book with Bruce D. Perry, *What Happened to You?* I love that title—a compassionate, kinder, and gentler alternative to "What's wrong with you?"

Add to this list, high achievers in every field: Olympic swimmer Michael Phelps, singer Adele, TV personality Stephen Colbert, actors Ryan Reynolds, Amy Poehler, Emma Stone, Leonardo DiCaprio, and even that ray of human sunshine, Kristen Bell. In her book *Bossypants*, Tina Fey wrote, "My ability to turn good news into anxiety is rivalled only by my ability to turn anxiety into chin acne." If the funniest woman in the world wrestles with fear, the rest of us can take comfort knowing we're all on the mat together. Gymnast Simone Biles became an Olympic gold medallist by twisting and turning her body, but at the Japan games in 2021, she took herself out of the competition when she realized the gymnastics of her mind were getting in the way of her performance and threatening her safety. She stunned the crowd by disqualifying herself, but I was profoundly moved by her decision; I knew she would end up helping so many more people by this demonstration of vulnerability than she would by standing atop the podium. She didn't take home a medal, but she showed her mettle with this courageous move.

All this to reiterate a simple fact: you are not alone. But your reptilian brain doesn't want you to know that, because your Gator relies on you feeling isolated so he can dominate you. That sense of isolation fosters more fear, and it also spawns secrecy.

Here's where it starts to get personal for me.

For a long time, I lived my life with a dark hole beneath me, the pit where my fear dwelled. Even when I became aware of it, I tried to deny it was there, convincing others and even myself it didn't exist. My life was perfect. My life was perfect. I was confident and outgoing. I was a deliriously happy wife and mother. I loved my job. That all sounds great, doesn't it? Unfortunately, every one of those statements is false.

I was false.

The truth was, my life was pretty wonderful, but I was not happy in it. I was too busy struggling with the huge cracks in my confidence while projecting an image to the world of a woman who had it all together. And since I was on television every night broadcasting to an audience of hundreds of thousands of people, that literal projection went far and wide. When I look back now, I had all the ingredients for a wonderful life, but there was no heat in the oven to bake the cake. There was something missing, but it wasn't anything I could put my finger on. And as my life grew, the crater beneath me grew as well. Fear was calling my name. And its voice was getting more persistent. I was going to have to stop running away and dig deep to find out what it had to say.

DIG

---

*"The only thing that will keep you from finding
that which you seek is calling off the search."*

—Rumi

I
t may seem paradoxical to be digging into the past in a book
largely devoted to the practice of being present, but as I've discovered, it can be powerful to get present with the past. Dig up
what's buried and look at it. Examine it like it's an archaeological
find. Digging up these pieces of the past and putting them back
together was the only way to get to know my true self—and to
understand how, and why, fear was interfering in my life.

As the lead archaeologist on this metaphorical dig, I had to dis-
play courage in excavating my fear. As I quickly learned, sometimes when you dig deep, mudslides happen. That's the best way
I can describe how my old impostor syndrome has been activated
during the writing of this book. In fact, one day when I was driving
to my cottage for a self-imposed lockdown to get some concen-
trated work done, I caught myself in this mudslide of thoughts:
*Why would anyone be interested in my personal story? Who the hell
do I think I am?* and *What delusional thinking has led me to believe I
have the ability to become an author?!*

Here's where the practice of presence comes in. I recognized this old pattern—and knew immediately that I had to airlift myself out of this avalanche of shit. Then I started to laugh. As I continued driving, I called my editor. When she answered, I let her in on the joke. "You're gonna love this," I exclaimed. "I'm on my way to a writing retreat, and I just caught myself slipping into impostor syndrome about writing a book about impostor syndrome!" She chuckled immediately, but it was a knowing laugh. Then she spouted some wisdom that calmed me down and set me straight: "That, my dear Nancy, is why you are the perfect person to write this book!" She reminded me of something I had forgotten. That the only thing I'm preaching is *practice*. The practice of presence.

In recent years I have realized how many people go through a very similar journey to my own. And furthermore, reading other people's books has taught me that when we share our personal stories, we allow others the opportunity to see themselves in our experiences. I learned that first-hand, reading books by Elizabeth Lesser, Dr. Edith Eger, Marianne Williamson, Elizabeth Gilbert, Michael Singer, Anne Bérubé, Wayne Dyer, and Glennon Doyle— to name just a few. To help myself over my self-created psychological hurdles, I decided to think of the following not as my story, but *a* story. One that has some good lessons about overcoming the fear of life. If it was someone else's story, I would be eager to have them share what they'd learned, so I'm going to throw myself into this hole with abandon in the hope that it will be useful to you.

And now, in order to share, I've got to get bare.

MY MASK

As the brilliant Dr. Brené Brown teaches, true connection requires authenticity. And authenticity requires vulnerability. So, since authenticity is what I'm digging for in this pit, being vulnerable is a necessary part of the adventure. For me, that means taking off my mask. The mask I've been sporting for a lifetime. The same mask that helped me pretend the hole beneath me wasn't there for so many years. The mask that enabled me to convince audiences that I was relaxed, enthusiastic, and confident, when I was desperately hiding my anxiety and a severe allergy to rejection. That mask served as my personal marketing for the brand that was *Nancy Regan*. But it was also my armour. And here's where we really dig into the distinction between Showing Off and Showing UP.

For far too many years I was living my life according to the expectations of others—which is, at best, a superficial existence and at worst, "life as performance art"—whether in front of an audience or one-on-one. Always trying to win approval. By relentlessly searching in the outside world for something that could only be found within, I was Showing Off. Showing UP, on the other hand, would have meant dropping the mask and allowing the world to see the real me.

What was I so afraid of?

Most of us start learning to show off almost from infancy. "Say cheese!" We're coached to "smile!"—paste a pleasant look on our face to show the world how cute, how good, how well-behaved we are. Projecting that we're living our best lives becomes our norm. These days, the equation is well established on social media: take a ton of photos, curate the best version of ourselves, then share.

This thought triggers a memory from my childhood. In my family, we had to be herded every autumn for our annual Christmas card. It was a high-stakes shoot with a renowned photographer, because we were under more pressure than the average family. My father was the premier of Nova Scotia from the time I was four until I was twelve. That meant that our family's holiday photo would land in every mailbox in the province. It's funny now to think back at the chaos behind the scenes, trying to corral six kids and get them to look presentable. There were layers of angst presented by time concerns, sibling conflicts, and the need to get it right—to get that perfect picture that showed the world what a lovely family we were. This was part of our marketing in the world of politics. If that photo had been the "live" kind that we have today, accompanied by a three-second video clip, it would not have supported the serene scene mailed to constituents every December.

I think we all had moments like this growing up; early life experiences that taught us to put on a happy face. To create a mask that would demonstrate to the world that we are worthy of approval. Unfortunately, all too often that veneer becomes indispensable as we age. And no wonder; if we had to put on the mask to thrive (or even survive), we start to believe things will fall apart if we take it off.

My parents were loving and supportive, and our home was comfortable and safe, and at times, full of fun. But like most other homes, there were also elements of stress, conflict, and of course consequences when my siblings and I stepped out of line. It may have been the day of free-range kids, but the flip side of that coin was that when we were with adults, children of my generation were subject to a lot of expectations—for behaviour, manners, and achievement—both at home and in school. In a house full of kids, I always felt a hunger for attention. In elementary school, gold stars became my obsession. But they were hard to come by at home. My dad's political career consumed a lot of my parents' time and energy.

Of course, my belief that I had to perform the role of Perfect Child in order to be worthy of my parents' love is not unique. In fact, it seems to be the universal scar of my generation. My story may well be your story. Performance was closely monitored, and any feedback I received (both negative and positive) taught me how to further craft my personality and behaviour. My constant goal was to procure praise and avoid punishment. It felt like attempting to cultivate, and then control, a garden full of invasive weeds.

It's crucially important to me to say that this is not parent-bashing. To some extent, constant course-correction was simply the way parenting was done then. It occurred to me recently that this was a clear example of the difference between implying and inferring. I honestly don't believe my parents ever implied that I was insufficient. Instead, it was a slow and steady inference I made. And it led to interference in my own sense of self.

So I set out to do everything I could to not be "bad." To show the world, and myself, that I was good. To present as the Perfect Child, belying my own knowledge that I was irretrievably flawed; I was loud in a world that valued quiet and polite children; I was distractable in a world that revered focus—and don't even get me started on my chronically messy bedroom. It was clear: I was lazy, inattentive, and disorganized, and these were things to be ashamed of.

Politics provided a privileged life. It also gave me an early education in the importance of popularity. The stakes are high when you need to be liked to get elected. To some extent I grew up in a fishbowl, so I guess it started to feel like my natural habitat (and I'd eventually find myself in a bigger one, on television). Everywhere we went as a family people recognized and watched us, and the understanding was implicit: we were being judged.

Most people I know grew up haunted by the question "What will the neighbours think?" But when you're living a public life, *everyone* is your neighbour, so that sense of needing to fit in and measure up is amplified. In my life, this concern burrowed so deep into my psyche it's earned itself a retroactive abbreviation: WWTNT. I grew up knowing that your whole life could depend on people liking and voting for you. And I wasn't a first-generation "prop."

My mother's father had been a Member of Parliament for Saskatchewan, so she had also grown up with that awareness of needing to please. When my brother Geoff was sworn in as Speaker of the House of Commons, Prime Minister Justin Trudeau stood up to make the ceremonial welcome and offer congratulations. After his introductory line, he paused and said, "To my knowledge, Mr. Speaker, there are only two women in Canada..." He left this hanging for a second with his customary dramatic flair. (I'm sure I wasn't the only one who had no idea where he was going.) But then the payoff: "...who have the dubious distinction of having been the daughter, wife, and mother of a Member of Parliament. One of them is, of course, my mother. The other, Mr. Speaker, is yours, and I'd like to pay tribute to her as she is in the gallery today." He motioned to my mom, who was sitting with my father. What happened next was even more unexpected. The whole House rose and gave my mother a standing ovation. I was watching the proceedings live on television from home, and I had tears in my eyes. When I asked Geoff's assistant later if my mother had been emotional about it, he surprised me by saying,

"No, it was your dad who couldn't stop tearing up!" My father had been deeply touched by this show of respect for a woman who had supported him through a lifetime of ups and downs. I have a lot of empathy for my mother, pondering how suffocating these life-long expectations must have been. She certainly stepped up to meet them, though—becoming a gracious host, a brilliant campaigner, and a genuinely compassionate citizen.

I've been asked many times through the years why I haven't gone into politics, and I usually quip that I served my time when I was a child. Only I'm not kidding. Because I was young, I had it a lot easier than some of my older siblings who had to navigate junior high and high school with the label "Premier's kid," but I still have some unpleasant memories. For one, there were the dreaded phone calls. We only had a landline in those days and our number was listed in the phone book. I had the unfortunate experience as a child of occasionally being on the other end of the abusive tirades of drunken disgruntled voters.

Most vivid in my memory, though, is the night of the garbage brigade. There was a huge controversy brewing at the time about where the county's new landfill should go, and the small town of Bedford (where we lived) was the prime contender. One night, a posse of angry residents snuck onto our property and dumped a huge load of garbage all over our lawn. I have a visceral memory of waking up to the alarmed shouts of my father and older brothers. Caught in the act, the intruders beat a hasty retreat. As an anxious child, I was shaken and scared, but I didn't allow anyone to know that at the time. When I think back, I can still see the heaps of litter that covered our yard the next morning. In fact, I could never see past them to run for politics.

As a child living in the public eye, I was intimately aware that my masked self was the one I was to show the public. And like many of us, I got so used to wearing it, it became a crutch. The division between my masked self and my real self was disappearing. I didn't realize it then, but I was learning to Show Off.

PERFECTIONISM

I learned the hard way that peeling off your mask is complicated. If you leave it on long enough, it becomes part of you. Or at least, it feels that way. In my experience, it's a lot like stripping layers of Varathane off an antique table, or chipping through packed stone with a spoon. Looking back now, I understand why. I didn't need strings to keep my mask on—it was glued on with an adhesive called *perfectionism.*

But I've got to stop now and make sure we're clear about what I mean by this term. Colloquially, we talk about perfectionism as simply striving to do one's best. I'm talking about clinical perfectionism, which comes with a dark side. Here's how it's defined by the website *GoodTherapy.org*:

> Perfectionism is often seen as a positive trait that increases your chances of success, but it can lead to self-defeating thoughts or behaviours that make it harder to achieve goals. It may also cause stress, anxiety, depression, and other mental health issues.

I realize now that I received a well-rounded education in perfectionism from some impeccable role models. Take, for instance, my piano teacher in elementary school. Her last name was Lightfoot, but she had a heavy hand. If it wasn't perfect, it wasn't good enough. Every week I'd show up, grudgingly but politely, for

In her book *A Return to Love*, Marianne Williamson says, "Our childlike self is the deepest level of our being. It is who we really are and what is real doesn't go away." I agree with her assessment that it doesn't go away, but it can get buried pretty deeply beneath layers of protection. And for me, that protection led to perfection— or rather the impossible *pursuit* of perfection. According to the Anxiety Canada website, perfectionism "involves a tendency to set standards that are so high they either cannot be met or are only met with great difficulty." For this reason, "perfectionists tend to believe that anything short of perfection is horrible, and that even minor imperfections will lead to catastrophe." While most people might be able to move on from their failures or believe the occasional mistake is understandable, people with perfectionism "tend to believe that they should never make mistakes and that making a mistake means they are a failure or a horrible person for disappointing others." When it comes to describing this ghastly affliction, I don't think anybody's nailed it like Elizabeth Gilbert, who wrote in her book *Big Magic*, "Perfectionism is just a high-end, haute couture version of fear...just fear in fancy shoes and a mink coat, pretending to be elegant when actually it's just terrified."

Fear in fancy shoes. That was me on *Live at 5*—fear I had everyone fooled; that I wasn't smart or talented enough. Fear that I wasn't...enough. If you happen to live on the east coast of Canada and remember me from my fifteen years co-hosting the CTV supper-hour show, this admission might surprise you. In fact, you might even find it hard to believe. After all, I appeared relaxed. I projected an air of confidence. But my internal reality was very different. As the co-pilot of this daily live-television broadcast, I felt eyes on me at all times—on-air and off. Over three hundred thousand nightly viewers might not top the charts for CNN, but in our small corner of the world, this kind of audience was enormous. It translated to what's known in TV ratings lingo as over a "50 share." That meant simply that at five o'clock each day, of all the television sets in the region that were turned on, over 50 percent were tuned in to our program. Living in that kind of spotlight presented some real psychological challenges for me, but I managed to conceal this from our viewers.

On live TV, I had an earpiece moulded to my ear, and it delivered a constant stream of chatter while I was speaking or interviewing a guest. At any time, the director might be telling me to switch to another camera. The technical producer might be informing me that our camera downtown had cut out, so we'd just lost my co-host who was live on location. Or the producer might be saying that the next story wasn't ready, so we'd need to rearrange our show. I will assure you that it takes a special skill set to pay attention to all these simultaneous messages while appearing focused and engaged on camera. But I had some experience with this, because I had lived with a voice in my ear for most of my life. And being on TV had turned up the volume on this one: *"That was a stupid thing to say." "Oh my God, you made another mistake!" "What are you doing here? You do not deserve this job."* Who do you suppose was perpetrating this emotional abuse? You guessed it. It was GUS, the voice of my fear. The fear of making mistakes, the fear of appearing stupid or unprepared. The fear of failing.

And that, my friend, is what was in the hole I was desperate to hide from.

———————————

No wonder I felt like an impostor. I had been hired as a summer reporter straight out of my English degree at St. Francis Xavier

University at age twenty-two. The only formal broadcasting training I got was on the job—in front of hundreds of thousands of people. "Are you crazy?!" had been my instinctive response when the executive producer asked me to audition for the co-host position on *Live at 5*. I remember him raising an eyebrow and chuckling, "That's probably not the right answer!" He had expected me to be excited, thrilled even. But I still hadn't fully absorbed the fact that I was working on the most popular TV news show east of Montreal.

The timeline explains why. In March of 1988, I was completing my final year of university, and in the process of changing gears. I had been sure I wanted to be an English teacher, but that goal lost its lustre when I became intrigued by the possibility of TV broadcasting. I had MCd a multicultural fashion show in Halifax the summer before that ended up being featured in a brief TV segment, and I got rave reviews. I liked the way the spotlight made me feel—like I was special, like I mattered, like I had something to say—so I headed straight for its glow.

A family friend helped me get in to see Dick Prat, the news director at ATV, the CTV affiliate in the Maritimes. I was there on a mission to get advice and direction. Should I go to journalism school, choose a program specifically geared toward broadcasting, or should I try to break into the business through a small radio station and work my way up? Dick Prat sized me up, apparently fell for my well-honed act of confidence, and floored me by saying, "Well, why don't we give you an audition and see what kind of potential you have." *Gulp.*

I told him I would love that, and then promptly lied through my teeth to save my life. "Unfortunately, I have another commitment now." I didn't, but I was terrified by his suggestion, and I had the presence of mind to postpone. I offered to make myself available any time that was good for him. Luckily for me, he agreed, and we settled on a day the following week. He explained the audition would entail my rewriting some scripts and doing a camera test. I headed straight back to St. FX, but I didn't do much schoolwork that week. My boyfriend at the time, Andrew Lively, played a big role in getting me ready and convincing me I could do this. Together, we tracked down news stories which I practiced rewriting. He then used his tape recorder to capture my voice as I rehearsed my delivery. Andrew served as coach, teammate, and cheerleader all wrapped into one supportive package.

To make a long story short, I went back to ATV the next week as planned, met with the executive producer, Harris Sullivan, and did my audition. He was kind and generous with his time, and really positive about my first attempt. I was invited back the following week for another audition. Then, another. On my third visit, Harris sat me down and told me I had a ton of potential. "I'd love to hire you as a summer reporter," he said, "but I can't justify doing that since I have all these people across the country who have experience and want the job." As he said this, he gestured to several huge stacks of ¾-inch videotapes. Then he made a proposition I couldn't refuse: If I wanted to come back after graduation the next month, I could work for free for a while and he would train me. I had planned to go backpacking in Europe with my cousin, but this was a once-in-a-lifetime chance. Although I marvel now at my guts and gumption, it was like I had gotten on a high-speed train and there was no jumping off.

I worked as an intern for about a month, and I guess I made a good impression because then...they put me on the air! I ended up getting one of those summer-replacement positions after all, and less than two months out of university, I was working as a reporter on *Live at 5*. Two months later, a new rival TV station launched and sent my brand-new career hurtling into warp speed. Many employees at ATV at the time chose to leave for what they likely saw as greener pastures, and included in that exodus was Laura Lee Langley, the popular female co-host of the five o'clock show. That's when Harris, who was clearly an out-of-the box creative thinker, decided to back me as her replacement. I was fortunate to be paired with Steve Murphy who was a seasoned pro by that time even though he was only twenty-eight (he looked forty then, as he did until he retired at sixty-one!). It's also important to mention Dave Wright and Bill Jessome, who were like the proverbial two old guys in the balcony of the Muppets show. Their dry humour made the newsroom a fun place to be, and they were extraordinarily supportive of their young colleagues.

Looking back now, in the context of the Black Lives Matter movement, the story of how my career got started is a powerful example of white privilege: I got my foot in the door because I knew people who knew people. In many ways, my experience represents the perpetuation of the white elite. I wouldn't grasp the nuances of this until decades later. But even though I fully acknowledge that I was part of an exclusive club, at the time I didn't feel I belonged there.

THE MAKING OF THE MASK

I was as green as the grass when I started on *Live at 5*, and I feel ridiculously fortunate to have been given the opportunity. But for me, it was a psychological minefield. I already cared too much what others thought of me, and stepping into this spotlight took that concern to a whole new level. Don't get me wrong, I loved hosting the show. In many ways, it was a dream job. In my fifteen years at the helm, I had exhilarating experiences, from broadcasting live from the red carpet at the Oscars to flying in a T-bird, to dancing on stage with the lead singer of the Beach Boys. I interviewed some of the biggest celebrities in the world. I sat on Oprah Winfrey's set in Chicago, interviewing *her*! But I did it all with my good friend fear riding shotgun. They say that courage isn't being fearless; it's being scared and doing it anyway. That pretty much sums up my story. But to say fear was my friend is misleading, because back then fear was my nemesis.

Watching the *Friends* reunion show recently with my daughter, I was struck by what Matthew Perry (Chandler) had to say about his time as a cast member on one of the most popular TV shows of all time. The world already knew about his struggles with addiction, but he addressed the monster that had been lurking beneath those challenges: his well-disguised anxiety. He was the guy with the zingers, but apparently that came with extra pressure: "I would sometimes say a line and they wouldn't laugh and I would sweat and just go into convulsions if I didn't get the laugh I was supposed to get. I would freak out...To me, it felt like I was gonna die if they didn't laugh. And it's not healthy, for sure." He covered it so well, not even his castmates knew he felt this way. I think I can say the same about my own co-workers. Most importantly though, the audience never knew how I really felt. They couldn't see my spiral of self-doubt. I loved theatre as a teenager, and I had learned to harness that acting ability in real life. I could *act* confident and everybody seemed to buy it. I'm living proof you can fake it till you make it, and I was a better actor than anyone ever knew.

But here's the other thing I loved about that job: the applause. It fed the hunger for praise that had been stoked in my childhood.

Don't love me because I'm special
Don't love what I achieve
Gold stars
Cause scars
And forge the need to please

Love me for who I am
In my deepest darkest heart
A fearful fraud
Simply flawed
Trying to be smart

See that, and see my light
The beauty of my soul
Just like you
Trying to get through
This journey back to Whole

My perfectionism developed early. It probably started when I occasionally saw my older siblings getting in trouble. I certainly didn't want any of that. I only wanted shiny stars and pats on the back! My mother had inherited her own mother's precise way of doing things, and that meant I was often corrected, even when doing the simplest tasks—like wrapping gifts for her. She was constantly attending gatherings for which hostess gifts were considered essential, and I remember doing a lot of wrapping. And unwrapping. And wrapping again. Properly.

It's so funny to think about how a memory as simple as this can surface when I consider the roots of my perfectionism. I can also conjure up the vivid memory of a seemingly endless etiquette session with my maternal grandmother. It was 1976, and I was ten. Queen Elizabeth and Prince Philip were visiting Nova Scotia and I was invited to a luncheon. Our family would also have the opportunity to meet and have our photos taken with the royal couple. Exciting, right? Not for this little tomboy. First of all, I had to be taken shopping for a significant item for which I had absolutely no use: a dress. And apparently, we couldn't chance Her Majesty seeing my rugged hands, so I needed white gloves, too. (As it turns out, this was compulsory attire for all females in attendance, but given my nail-biting habit, it was probably for the best!)

In the days preceding the royal luncheon, I was sequestered in our sunroom for what seemed like hours on end. I don't recall any of my siblings having to go through this, so either I was the worst-mannered or I have selective memory. Either way, there I was, trapped by the most particular grandmother I knew (and the only one I had)—and her roots were showing. Her British roots, that is. This was serious business, and I can't help but laugh now at how hard she had to work to bring me up to snuff! By the end of that chapter, I was ready for the Etiquette Olympics. Sit me down at any table now, and I can identify the proper fork to employ for the correct course. All these years later, I'm appreciative of Gran's efforts, but I sure look back on my time playing cards with her with a lot more fondness.

What I've discovered in the years since, is that perfectionism is not merely a personality trait. It's like a glitch in your programming. It prevents the smooth running of your life. As I tell my presentation clients, speaking in front of others is a complicated business—*because we're not robots*. Instead of efficient processors, we humans come equipped with brains. They tend to be unpredictable, imperfect organs that are prone to viruses—thought viruses! So, as helpful as our brains can be, they can also be a hindrance to our daily functioning. And to really understand how our own thought processes work, we need to dig deep into the hole of our deepest, darkest fears. And part of that involves reckoning with our past. Hold onto your hat now, because there's a lot to unpack here. And to really unzip this baggage, let's go back a few more years, to when I was eight.

SHOWING UP

There I am now: walking out the door to school. I'm wearing polka-dot pants and a striped top. "There goes my little Orphan Annie," says my mom. I never understood what that meant, but it rolled off me like water off a duck's back. Of course, I know now that she was marvelling, in good humour, at my lack of style, and I'm sure from her perspective I went out into the world looking like I had no mother to dress me. But that was my happily dorky self—the same one it took me half a lifetime to find again.

Remember the story of the Ugly Duckling? My journey followed a similar narrative through the rocky landscape of appearance. In most pictures of my childhood, I look like a boy. In fact, people sometimes mistook me for one when I was out with my mother and younger brother. "What a sweet little boy and girl," they'd say. Only, they had it backwards. David, with his brown curls and gentle eyes, was mistaken for the girl. I was the boy. I had straight hair with just enough wave to look like bedhead. To further the confusion, I was devoted to wearing slacks, as my mom called them, and had to be wrestled into a skirt when occasions called for "appropriate attire."

That was my own fashion sense (or lack thereof) declaring itself. I was comfortable in those clothes, and they were well suited to my preferred pastimes: playing outside (games like Mother-May-I and Red Rover), creating pine-needle forts, and generally running the roads. I look back at those old photos now as a beautiful chapter, because I had yet to become aware of my "girlish deficits." I was proud that I could fit my whole thumb behind my outrageous over-bite—with my teeth closed. Enough people had called me a tomboy by then that I'd simply accepted it and moved on. At age eight, it didn't matter to me that I wasn't a "girly girl," but as I got older, the world sent me plethora of messages telling me to change. To morph into a clearer expression of a female.

Barbie may have had something to do with that.

Incongruent as it might seem, I loved playing Barbies with my friends, but my fascination with Mattel's bombshell had more to do with her boyfriend, Ken. I enacted endless romantic scenarios for the plastic couple. While I may have looked boyish, the earliest hints of my sexual preference were clear. And a boy named Scott B was the apple of my eye. He was the son of my mother's hair-dresser, and as our moms became friends, Scott and I got to spend lots of time together. I may have been only eight, but I was madly in love. Who could blame me? He had blond hair, blue eyes, and classic good looks. He had a quick smile and an open spirit. Come to think of it, he was a mini version of my tv crush, Steve Austin. (I'm sure I wasn't the only fan who fell in love with the Six Million Dollar Man!) But alas, my infatuation was a one-way street. I vividly remember daydreaming about being kissed by him, fantasizing about revealing my feelings to him. How he'd be surprised, but happy. Maybe even thrilled. To my everlasting disappointment, I never had the confidence to declare my affection.

Even then, I had some awareness of my awkwardness, as if I was still walking through life in the ugly brown Oxford shoes that had adorned my feet in my earliest days. I was born pigeon-toed, and that had to be corrected. I hated those shoes with a passion, but the doctor and my parents made it clear that my inwardly turned feet had to be straightened.

I really had no thought of ever being attractive until one day in grade three, when Shelley H changed my life. "My mom says you're going to be beautiful someday," she said in a bemused sort of way. "Because you've got high cheekbones." This newsflash nearly knocked me off my feet. In fact, it's one of those memory-snippets that are so clear, you can see where you were when it happened—like the Kennedy assassination and the moon landing, this felt like it had similar import in my young life. But could it really be *true*?

Those Oxford shoes never did fix my feet. Watch me walk in an unguarded moment these days and you'll agree. But the orthodontics did fix my teeth. In fact, even before the braces were done working their magic on my jaw, the shifting of the bones in my face triggered a shift in the world's reaction to me. Actually, it felt more like an earthquake. I was thirteen, and in the midst of morphing from dorky to slightly less dorky during my second year at summer camp, I discovered the transformative phenomenon of the *male gaze*.

His name was Bruce, he was from a different part of the province, and I suppose he looked enough like Scott B to be my type. But what really made him appealing was that he showed an interest in *me*! (No wonder Camp Wapomeo quickly became my favourite place on Earth.) My first kiss is as vivid in my memory as Shelley H's pronouncement. It happened after our nightly campfire. Hunky Bruce and his friend were seated on the wooden benches of the rec hall with me and my new friend Susan from New Glasgow. The romance of the scene was fostered by the magic of all our voices raised in song, the sense of fun created by our cool teenaged counsellors, and the heady independence of being away from home. I don't recall who paired up with Susan that night, but I can still feel my hand in Bruce's. There was an electricity that flowed through that innocent physical connection, and it was amplified exponentially when he walked me back to my cabin and kissed me goodnight.

It was just one quick kiss, but I was fully charged by the time I stepped inside. I have a clear recollection of pulling my duffel bag out from beneath my bunk while we girls debriefed. (I think of this every time I see *Grease*—"Tell me more" was the phrase of the night.) Caught up in the chatter, I took out my pyjamas, unfolded them, and then promptly refolded them and placed them absent-mindedly back in my bag. My discombobulation was met with gales of laughter, but what I realize now is that my status changed that night. I was a girl who had a boy who liked me. And that meant something to the other girls. It also meant an enormous amount to me. It opened a door to a new type of approval; one that I would grow to crave.

I've never considered myself particularly ambitious, but as a child, I did have one distinct ambition: to get attention. From the beginning, growing up in a house with six kids and two busy parents, I'd used my voice to get noticed, so it's highly appropriate that it would end up earning me a living. Looking at our old family films, I can see my life force in full bloom, but there's also evidence of my hunger for the spotlight. I basically invented the "photobomb." How annoying my persistent need for attention must have been to my older siblings. They used to bribe me on road trips, offering me money if I could stop talking for five minutes. (For the record, I couldn't!) The phrase "shut up!" was not allowed within our parents' earshot, but they were out a lot, and I heard it enough that the echo remains.

Ironically, though, my voice earned me a big dose of approval the first time I read in public. I can go there instantly in my mind: St. Ignatius Church, an edifice to which I was dragged bodily on a weekly basis. I have two distinct memories of these services: fear that my mother might quiz me afterwards about the content of the homily, and an awareness of my own growth—and I'm not talking spiritually. During Catholic Mass, there are several points at which the congregation is expected to kneel, and every Sunday when we slid our bums off the bench and lowered our knees to the cushioned tuffet—*Just like Miss Muffet's*, I remember thinking—I got busy taking stock of how much I had grown since the week before.

I felt so small and insignificant when everyone around me could rest their elbows on the back of the pew in front of us, while I had to stretch my little arms up to even hook my fingers over the top. It was so exciting when my eye level rose above the wooden horizon and I could see glimpses of the altar without standing up. And when I got tall enough that I could rest my own elbows on that ledge with an almost perpendicular arm, this weekly commitment seemed more tolerable.

As I said, I don't recall experiencing much *spiritual* growth during that chapter of my life, but I know it laid some kind of groundwork for a connection to spirit. Although I wryly refer to myself these days as a "recovering Catholic," when I attend a Mass now, whether for a wedding or funeral, I often feel nostalgic for that sense of community. Community in silence, in stillness. Not unlike the profound online connection felt by so many of us during the lockdown in the first phase of the pandemic.

The first day I read aloud from the church lectern, I experienced instant gratification. The positive feedback was like my first hit of a drug to which I'd soon become addicted. *"What a fabulous voice you have." "You speak so beautifully." "You should do this more."* This was the opposite of being told to shut up, and it felt good. And so, the seeds were planted. *As you sow, so shall you reap.*

I began searching out the spotlight.

I got my first taste of acting with a lead part in a play put on by my Brownies troupe. I realize now that my tomboy nature might have played a role in the casting choice, because I portrayed the founder of the Guiding movement, Lord Baden-Powell. I did a good job, by all accounts, even managing to roll with the punches when my moustache dislodged itself halfway through my biggest scene. It fell onto the stage, but I stayed impeccably in character as I casually swept it up and attempted to paste it back above my upper lip. All this while continuing with my lines. There may have been a few giggles from others, but I was in the moment. "Play" is all about presence. (In fact, we'll go into this a bit more in the Doorways to Presence.)

I would find other stages as I got older. Throughout my teens, basketball was something I excelled at, and loved. I was living in Ottawa when, in my final year of high school, I was chosen for the city All-Star team and my school team won the Ontario provincials. Despite this success, I opted not to try out for the varsity team when I arrived at university. Why? Good old-fashioned fear of failure. In a happy twist of fate though, taking a pass on varsity sport made space for drama, and I fell madly in love with acting on the dusty stage of St. Francis Xavier University's Bauer Theatre.

You might consider it odd that someone so insecure would be willing to step out into the spotlight, with the pressure of remembering lines and blocking moves, but in actual fact, this was an extraordinary escape from my negative mental chatter. Like playing an intense game of basketball, I had to be completely focused, so it forced me into the present moment. I didn't realize it then, but I was practicing presence. Because I was *acting*, I wasn't practicing it in any conscious way, but there was a freedom in this kind of playful performance, and I loved losing myself in the playwright's imaginary world.

A wonderful woman by the name of Addy Doucette was the director of all the plays I performed in at St. FX, and she recognized some natural talent in me. As it turns out, she's an avid gardener these days, and it occurs to me that she tended me like a flower. Her encouragement was my fertilizer, and under the stage lights I found the warmth I'd been craving. It lit me up, and made me feel like I was special. But like any addiction, it triggered a desire for more, and eventually a dependence.

I've seen enough interviews and talked to enough actors to know that my experience is not unique. Addiction to the spotlight is a classic path to the world of acting. It's also why so many actors who seem to have the world by the tail end up eventually revealing an inner life of insecurity and self-doubt. The penultimate example of this is the huge ego that hides small self-esteem, the tired old act of someone of profile throwing their weight around: "Don't you know who I *am*?!"

I speak from experience when I describe the unanticipated pitfalls of fame. Everywhere you go, people communicate the message that You Are A Big Deal. That you matter more than others. That you're exceptional. Two things happen simultaneously: on one level of consciousness, you buy into that marketing job and allow it to bolster you; but on another level, you feel a deeply unsettling knowledge that it's just not true. You are the Wizard of Oz.

SHOWING OFF

One day recently, I was in my kitchen making supper while watching a documentary about the making of the show *Schitt's Creek*. It's an award-winning comedy about an obscenely wealthy family who has lost their fortune and landed, penniless, in a small rural town; a true fish-out-of-water tale. In discussing the various elements he believed had made the show a hit, show creator and star Dan Levy made a comment about the production's costuming that immediately got my attention:

> Wardrobe is probably the most important element in storytelling outside of writing because we, as people, say so much about who we are and what we believe in, and what we want, and what we think of ourselves, by the way that we dress.

He was talking about his decision to use actual high-fashion pieces when dressing his actors. He wanted the clothes to look legit, not like knockoffs pretending to be "designer." (Imagine the wardrobe department's delight when they discovered they'd be working with clothes right off the runway!) A few moments later,

Catherine O'Hara, who plays Dan's mother in the show, voiced her agreement: "When you get these kind of clothes on, you just feel different. You stand differently, you move differently, people look at you differently, and I feed off of all that."

In my presentation-training work, there's a lesson in this in terms of creating an impression on stage, but since this is a book based on the power of presence, first we have to deconstruct it. It's one thing to be an actor consciously constructing a character or a speaker cultivating an air of authority, but so many of us get wrapped up in the construction of our own "characters," which we wear like disguises out in the world.

How do we want others to see us? What opinion would we like people to have of us? How can we create a positive impression of ourselves in the minds of others? Being constantly concerned with questions like these leads us to assemble what I think of as a mask. And staying in the world of TV and movies for a moment, who better to address the concept of a mask than the guy who made millions off a movie of the same name?

Jim Carrey is one of the most successful movie stars of all time. His films have grossed over $2 billion, but in the past decade Carrey has had what he describes as "an awakening." In the documentary *Jim & Andy: The Great Beyond,* he tells the story of his obsessively realistic portrayal of comedian Andy Kaufman in the 1999 film *Man on the Moon.* He also gets personal and talks about the process of creating a persona as a successful actor; having to decide between relinquishing your dependence on that mask and coming to terms with living out the rest of your life as someone other than yourself:

At some point, when you create yourself—to make it...
you're going to have to either let that creation go, and take
a chance on being loved or hated for who you really are, or
you're gonna have to kill who you really are...and fall into
your grave grasping onto a character that you never were.

For many years, I crafted a character according to what would
win me admiration, adding layers that would eventually need
to be peeled off. This seems like a perfect time to tell you about
my Miss Canada 1987 experience. I came across a YouTube video
of the pageant recently and I feel a little nauseous when I think
about it, for a couple reasons. Primarily, as a perfectionist, it was
my first big failure. Not only did I not win, I didn't even make it
into the top eight. *What a loser!* Ridiculous, right? But I actually
felt that way. So, there's a lingering discomfort when I remember
the experience, but a fresh feeling of shame permeates my being
as I watch it today.

The opening sequence switches back and forth between live
shots of forty-four contestants dancing and singing a song about
a dream—the gist of which is that *if we believe it, we can achieve
it.* Alternating with this montage are five-second close-up snippets of each of us saying our name and thanking our sponsors.
Most of the girls look like deer in the headlights for this moment
of national fame, though a few seem a little more comfortable.
We had been rehearsing this sequence for a week, and on the
actual broadcast, because it was the fortieth anniversary of the
pageant, we were joined by a bevy of Miss Canadas from years
past. Watching the video now, I'm struck by two things. The first
is that every one of those beauty queens was standing in just the
way my mother had tried to coach me as a girl: one foot turned

outward to eleven o'clock, and the heel of the other foot tucked into the arch of the first foot, pointing to two o'clock. It's a stance that creates the illusion of slimmer hips, and every single former Miss Canada had gotten the memo. But the other thought that flashes through my head now is *Why didn't those older women warn us about the perils of the "beauty myth," or protect us from ourselves?*

My performance is, in a word, hideous. And this is not my perfectionist speaking. So much for all the people who advised me "Just be yourself!" The girl I see on the screen bears no resemblance to me. She has been coached to walk and talk a certain way; she's thinned down in order to feel less embarrassment about her thighs in a swimsuit; her hair is pulled back uncharacteristically in a high, tight bun because she's told she should show off her cheekbones, and there are approximately six pounds of makeup on her sweet young face. Worst of all, her delivery is totally fake. Far removed from my basketball sneakers and sweatpants, I am no longer the girl next door but the mannequin at the mall. I couldn't have been more out of my element.

I realize now this was the true beginning of my road to inauthenticity. Today, as I dig into the sense of mortification I feel at watching this performance, I realize those feelings are about my own self-betrayal; my willingness to accept this exchange—trading in who I really was for what I was told I was supposed to be. Don't get me wrong; when I breathe through it, I don't regret this chapter or resent it, because it ended up being a big part of my learning journey. And as you can see, I'm still learning! *Practice, practice, practice.*

It was a strange series of events that led to me being a pageant "queen." I had scored a sweet summer job working for our hometown recreation department with a friend, who ended up saddled with the job of organizing the Miss Bedford pageant. When only three girls signed up, my friend begged me and another acquaintance to enter, insisting it would look like a failure if the pageant had to be cancelled. In the end, we were convinced only because Cheryl J was to be one of the contestants. A stunning young woman who went on to be a successful international model, she was the clear winner. Or at least she should've been. As things turned out, I emerged the bewildered new owner of a sash and tiara.

Although I initially opted to take a pass on the provincial competition, my parents convinced me it was a good opportunity, and off I went that August to the Miss Nova Scotia pageant. I'm pretty sure no one was more surprised than me when I won. I didn't have to fake the shocked look on my face. The good news was, I had discovered pageants weren't so bad after all. I had made friends and experienced a rewarding sense of camaraderie. So I went off to the Miss Canada pageant with an optimistic enthusiasm. Only the national level turned out to be everything I had ever suspected: too many young women who had tunnel vision for the crown and were willing to do whatever it took to win it. I think this was when I really began to learn to Show Off instead of Showing UP. It also marks the life chapter in which beauty became my albatross.

I was attending St. FX during this chapter of my life, and between my "reign" as Miss Nova Scotia and my acting roles, I had unwittingly fashioned my own little fishbowl. I got a job with the campus police, possibly the best job ever. Here's what it entailed: walking around campus at night—typically paired with a male varsity athlete—wearing very cool vintage leather jackets with our designation emblazoned across the back. We would stop into the various social gatherings—sanctioned and otherwise—and deal with any shenanigans. We were first responders in a way. But there was a response I became accustomed to from my partners that drove me crazy. It would typically occur halfway through our evening shift, after we'd had a chance to chat and get to know each other as we did "the rounds."

"You're not a snob!" they'd say out of the blue, as if they'd made a startling discovery. I got used to hearing this, but the sting never went away. Invariably, they'd report that they'd heard I was "stuck up," but were happy to find that wasn't the case. Their verdict: "You're totally down to earth." But was I really? Or was that what I wanted them to see? The answer is, both.

Back in my first year at Camp Wapomeo, I had won the Best Camper award, and as I see it now, much of my life was spent campaigning for that kind of recognition. You've probably heard the phrase "triple threat." In the world of acting, it's used to describe someone who can act, sing, and dance. I think I was a triple threat in a different way; I knew how to *act* confident, but I also knew how to *be* approachable, and at heart I really was, and believe I still *am*, a good person. In a way, those early experiences giving weight to other people's judgements prepared me for the ultimate stage of live television, and the largest audience of my life.

LIES AT 5

As I aged and my insecurities mounted, my hunger for external praise grew alongside my fear of criticism, and my television job turned out to be a crucible for that perfect storm. Can you imagine a better fix for an approval junkie than literally standing in the spotlight in front of a camera? Everywhere I went, viewers approached me to let me know how much they loved my show, and me. On the east coast of Canada, we're renowned for our hospitality, but I experienced that friendliness on a whole other level. Anywhere I went in our region, I was greeted like a member of the family. What an extraordinary privilege that was! When I had my first baby, I was flabbergasted by the response. I received a deluge of homemade baby blankets, sweaters, and other gifts from complete strangers. Generous people who felt like they knew me.

But here's the thing; they only knew *part* of me.

When the Confederation Bridge opened, connecting PEI to the mainland, *Live at 5* did a live broadcast "on location." But what I remember most was the day before the actual opening. The Fixed Link, as it was known then, was a monumental milestone, and on opening day, May 31, 1997, it was open only to pedestrians. My co-host, Paul Mennier, and I set off on the 12.9-kilometre trek, eager to cross this impressive structure—the longest bridge in the world built across ice-prone water—and we were in good company. Thousands of people turned out that day. Come to think of it, this was probably the first time Paul and I had immersed ourselves in a crowd together—a crowd we could *see*. Of course, we were often out in public individually, and we were often out together while doing our remote broadcasts, but this time we were without the layers of insulation typically provided by our production crew. There is no science in this assessment, but I would estimate that, because we were walking as a pair, our recognition factor was tripled. We must've talked to half the people there that day. It was both enlivening and exhausting. But it wasn't the physical exercise that tired me out. We could barely make it ten metres without getting stopped. *"Oh my gosh, I love you guys!" "You eat dinner with us every night." "We love watching your show because you both clearly love your jobs so much."*

Of course, our viewers only knew the two-dimensional versions of Paul and me from their TV screens. Our professional selves. And on that day, like the island now attached to the mainland, we spent hours tethered to our avatars—those perfect versions of ourselves—showing up as the friendly, approachable, likable hosts we strove to be. Paul and I *were* all those things. A lot of the time. But interacting with an audience in this way, much like entertaining clients for those in business, can be draining because it's a type of performance. For me, it was the epitome of Showing Off. Moving through conversations as my filtered self, giving people what they expected. I was living up to others' expectations, but that wasn't enough for me. I had to win more approval. Compound approval— like interest. I wanted people to walk away feeling I was even nicer than they'd expected. I was down-to-earth and funny. I was not a "snob." This might have been partly professional branding, but for me it was also personal. On some level, I was seeking proof that I was lovable.

The filter I'm talking about had to be in place whenever we were on air. It was our job as hosts to make people feel relaxed, to entertain them, and to engage them with whatever tools we had to keep them watching. To increase our viewership. I remember hearing one time that Paul had a high "Q rating." This was a reflection that all segments of the audience liked and related to him. I don't remember ever being told how I "Q'd," and I avoided asking—because I didn't want to know. I couldn't handle the possibility that not everybody liked me. That would be failure.

It was bad enough they didn't like my hair.

It was actually carved into my contract that I couldn't change my hairstyle without permission from my bosses. I'm pretty sure this clause was not applied to male hosts, and it's one I bent repeatedly. When I left *Live at 5*, they did an entire show devoted to my time as co-host, and one of the hilarious highlights was a segment focused on my constantly shifting hairstyle. Viewed in a personal rear-view mirror, my hair was a symbol of a constant struggle for approval, but also a visual representation of my hustle to Show Off— to feel worthy of the part I was playing—because I wasn't comfortable enough to Show UP.

There were constant reminders of my need to look good, and to be popular. Like any job performance metrics in some ways, but outrageously amplified in others. I didn't just need to impress my employer and satisfy the terms of my contract. I literally had to be approved of by hundreds of thousands of viewers. The satisfaction of the audience was measured every spring and fall in ratings periods (talk about a 360-degree job review!). But I also got daily doses of unsolicited micro-feedback.

One time in a bar, a young guy approached me. He raved about how he loved watching me on TV, but sandwiched in the middle of all that positive evaluation, he casually inserted a slice of criticism. Without taking a breath or changing tone, he said, "I liked your hair better when it was long." This was the subtle message I got every day—that viewers had a right to judge me. I was in the public domain, and because I hosted a show they watched faithfully, their opinions should matter. The truth is, they did matter to me—too much.

The particular haircut he was referring to almost broke the switchboard. I was thirty-five, and I had cut my shoulder-length locks into a pixie cut. I knew enough to pop out to see our receptionist after my first show with the new coif. She looked beleaguered. In fact, she immediately announced that I owed her a drink, because she had spent the entire hour fielding calls from people who wanted to register their views on my change in appearance. "I've got good news and bad news," she said. "Half the people love it, but the other half hate it." This makes me chuckle now, but at the time it was hard to hear. I hadn't yet figured out that you can't please everyone all the time.

As much as I craved the warmth of the spotlight, its dark counterpart was scrutiny. And that's what led to my desperate fear of making mistakes. A few years into my career, I was tasked with introducing a famous motivational speaker who had come to Halifax to deliver a seminar. Our station was the primary sponsor of the full-day workshop and so, representing ATV, I was to welcome the crowd at the start of the event and introduce the star of the show.

I will never forget meeting Tony Robbins backstage on the Halifax Metro Centre. As I was led toward him, I realized he was the largest human I had ever encountered. He looked straight into my eyes, smiled broadly, and reached out his hand. My own hand felt like a child's in his. But it wasn't just his physical body that was huge (he's about 6'7"); he had the biggest presence of anyone I'd ever met. Energy exuded from his pores. He was confidence personified.

After my introduction, Tony strode out onto the stage like he owned it and his confidence and charisma filled the stadium. No obvious script or notes…he was just talking to the audience. It was a masterclass in stage presence. I was mesmerized, and so was the crowd. He had us in the palm of his huge hand. His own presence had rendered the audience present, too. This was something that would stay with me, and that I'd share with my presentation clients decades later.

Tony delivered a lot of messages that day, but one in particular was the most powerful and enduring to me. In hindsight, I realize it was my first invitation to presence. An invitation to actually delve into that dark hole I was trying to hide. Tony Robbins, one of the most successful speakers in the world, was up there on the stage talking about something I knew intimately: the fear of failure. And one particular statement triggered a realization in me: "Sometimes the security of a mediocre present is more comfortable than the adventure of trying to be more in the future." This pronouncement was a force hitting me square in the chest, waking me up to my own truth. I felt like I had been avoiding adventure as long as I could remember.

I immediately flashed back to high school; the vice principal was trying to convince me to run for president of the students' council. Several of my friends were pushing me too, but there was simply no way it was going to happen. You see, they seemed to think I was smart, confident, and popular, but I knew differently. I knew I had everyone fooled. I also knew that if I found myself in a position of "power" and responsibility, it would inevitably be revealed that I was an *impostor*. My most important job at that stage of my life was concealing my secret—that I was actually a complete dork. And despite my high-profile career and perceived success, that hadn't really changed over the years.

Now, here was this guy I'd never met before telling my story, precipitating a cascade of realizations—the main one being that I had been playing it safe for much of my adult life, steering clear of opportunities to broaden my horizons for fear of falling off the edge of the Earth as I knew it. But, wait a second...I was hosting a daily live television program with an enormous audience. How could both things be true?

Well, that's where paradox comes into the picture.

I received a lot of praise for my work on television, but it didn't swell my head. The constant stream of positive feedback actually just helped balance my own inner critic. It's important to understand that my mask was not opaque; it was transparent. People were seeing the real me, but only as I wanted to present myself. So, in my mind, they only liked me because they didn't see all of me. And that meant that often praise made me feel even more like an impostor. But more on that later. Right now, we've got a dark hole to explore, so let's keep digging!

———————

I put my mask to excellent use over my years on television. I was constantly being called on to do things well beyond my comfort level. But remember, failing wasn't an option, so I did it all with a smile on my face—and GUS chattering away in my head.

I did a lot of flying for work—even once experiencing the centrifugal force of 4 "Gs" in a sharp turn in an RCAF T-33 T-Bird—but I also *jumped out* of a perfectly good airplane for a two-part series in the midst of a summer story drought. This adventure involved four hours of training before heading up for my first sky-dive. I specify "first" because I jumped a total of three times that day. The first time, I left my cameraperson on the ground below and he got a terrific shot of my effortless landing. The second jump was easier because I had a perfect one under my belt. This time, my cameraperson was in a tandem aircraft, so he got a fantastic shot of my mid-air departure. I had to hold a stance in the open doorway of the plane until my instructor nodded his head and said, authoritatively, "Okay, Nancy, step away!" And step away I did. I was on my own, but my pack was equipped with a mini parachute that caught the air and triggered the release of the Velcro fasteners holding the main chute. So I didn't free fall for long.

I was more relaxed the second time I left that doorway, but it didn't last. My senses may have been overwhelmed on my first dive, but the second time I became more aware of the air currents buffeting me about. There's nothing quite like hitting an air pocket and going into free fall with nothing to catch you but hard ground far below. Suffice it to say I was much less excited for my third jump. This time my cameraperson was riding along in the same plane, so he could get shots of me bailing out from inside. I once again took my position in the frame of that damned door and felt the weight of my fear. GUS had apparently been hypnotized by my first jump but awakened by my second. And now he was freaking out, silently shrieking, "Don't do it again!"

I suddenly realized I didn't *need* to leap, and excitedly announced that we could cut from this static shot to the tandem angle of the actual jump. But my sky-dive coach didn't fall for it. He locked eyes with me and said, calmly but firmly, "Step away, Nancy." People pleaser that I was, off I went. In that moment, I wasn't considering my own safety or well-being, but what was *expected* of me. While I'm happy to report that it all ended well, after that hat-trick, I never felt the urge to dive out of the sky again.

Over my fifteen years on *Live at 5*, I found myself in many other situations that were far less dangerous but elicited an even stronger fear response. We regularly broadcast live from many locations across the Maritimes and beyond. In retrospect, I realize that when I was expected to follow a script without the safety of my studio teleprompter, I got super jittery about screwing up. But when I could break from the prescribed text to improvise in an interview, I was more able to relax and *be myself.*

Just six months after starting as co-host, I took part in the first-ever live news show to be broadcast in its entirety from Walt Disney World. Our whole team was there, and the show happened to land on my birthday. Mickey Mouse himself delivered a Disney-approved cake on air, but we didn't let our audience know I was only turning twenty-three. At the time, I was hyper-aware of any small mistakes I might make, but looking back on it now, I'm in awe that I managed to pull it off. It was sink or swim, and I swam like hell—not elegantly, but I managed to stay on the right side of the surface. (Considering it was Florida, it should be no surprise that GUS the Gator felt empowered!)

Five years later, we returned to the Sunshine State for a week-long series of live shows. Dubbed *Live at 5's Spring Fling,* I remember it as *Hell on Wheels.* First, because I was literally on wheels for the show opening on the Miami Beach boardwalk. It must have been Paul Mennier's idea to start on Rollerblades. He was an avid hockey player and solid on his skates. That turned out to be a blessing, since he had to physically catch me right before the live opening sequence when I almost went tail over teakettle. That rocky start was an omen of sorts, at the beginning of a challenging week during which I flung myself into a complete crisis of confidence.

Our producer had neglected to line up any shoots for me, and each day I struggled to find a story, then get it shot and edited in time for our broadcast, which was an hour earlier than usual. The biggest problem I encountered was that I had left my "neighbourhood," and fishbowl, behind. No one in Florida knew me, or my show, so there was no motivation to rearrange their day for an interview. So much for the *Fling* part; I was not having fun. That week, I realized that, in a way, my charmed life had been protecting me from rejection. It wasn't until we hit the west coast on day four and landed in St. Pete Beach that things improved. There were so many Maritime snowbirds there, it felt like we'd come home. Everyone wanted to talk to me!

My enduring memory of that week is the negative spiral of my self-belief. The more I obsessed about the small mistakes I made on air, the more I'd make. I put my acting skills to good use that week, on air and off. Little did my team know that I was on the verge of a panic attack during our live shows, hanging on by my fingernails. I've often wished I could go back and do it all over again without GUS riding shotgun. If I had been able to focus on the fun instead of the fear, it would've been a very different week.

Movie junkets were simultaneously a high and low of my job, but in order to explain why, I need to describe how they work. When promoting a new film, studios regularly fly entertainment reporters into a city (usually New York or LA) to facilitate a slew of interviews with the movie's stars, producers, and director. ATV got in on this action first with Paramount Pictures in the early 1990s and at the time was the only station representing the east coast of Canada. I loved the trips, and no wonder. Flying in the face of journalistic ethics, we junketeers were put up in the most luxurious hotels—often The Plaza in New York and The Beverly Hills Four Seasons in LA. The first evening, we'd be taken to a theatre nearby where we'd have a private screening of the film. I often enjoyed the movies, but I always got uptight before my interviews. None more so than for *Braveheart* (1995).

I was interviewing Mel Gibson. As the star, director, and producer of the film, he was at the top of his game. I had never been more nervous for an interview. I remember pacing the hallway of the Four Seasons like an expectant father. Amused and puzzled, my friend from Paramount asked me what was going on. "You do these all the time, Nancy. What are you so nervous about?" I looked at her dumbfounded, and said, "Um, it's *Mel*-frigging-*Gibson*!"

Once ushered in, I had, as usual, less than a minute to say hello to the star before I was suited up with a microphone. Gibson was sitting in a period velvet chair, and as I lowered myself into an identical one across from him, he asked how I was doing. For some bizarre reason, I dropped my mask momentarily and told the truth (or at least a version of it). "I'm a little nervous," I said, cringing internally. What happened next was magic. "Nervous of talking to me?!" he exclaimed. "I can fix that." He screwed up his handsome movie-star face into the goofiest look he could muster, hooked one finger into his mouth, and with the other hand, began slapping his face. Then, as quickly as he'd started, he stopped. He looked at me, smiled kindly, and said, "There! Do you feel better now?" I laughed, realizing that not only had I relaxed, but I had been reminded in that moment that we were both just human beings. And, although I didn't realize it at the time, he had helped prepare me for another giant interview: Oprah.

―――――――――――

Six months later, I flew to Chicago to do an exclusive interview with one of the most powerful women in showbiz (and perhaps in the world). But after my interaction with Mel, I had gained a little control over my nerves. I knew the stakes were high, but I also knew I was up to the challenge. I had a chance to get acclimatized my first day there, when I sat in the audience while the Queen of Talk recorded two episodes of *The Oprah Winfrey Show*. Then the next day, I sat on that stage with Oprah herself—with *me* asking the questions. It was surreal. And just like with Mel Gibson, a funny thing happened before we started rolling that really relaxed me.

Oprah and I were chatting as she munched on a veggie platter. I asked her if she had grown to love that kind of food. She replied in a hilarious way, making it clear her food choices were all about dieting. I was reminded, in her focus on weight, that she was just human, like me—and Mel! Then, as we were casually chatting while the cameras got set up, I was comfortable enough to allow a casual habit to surface. It was the nineties, when "Hello?!" had become a popular catchphrase. It was typically meant to express surprise or sarcasm in a funny way, and because Oprah's energy had put me at ease, it just slipped out. But instead of saying it in English, I laughingly interjected, "Bonjour?!" Oprah sat up straight and exclaimed, "I love that! I'm going to use that, Nancy!" And she did, later in our interview.

One of the hallmarks of a great interviewer is that they make the interviewee feel comfortable enough that their true personality can shine through. I was good at doing that in my role as host, and constantly heard from people with whom I'd just finished recording, "Oh, you made that so much easier than I expected it would be!" That day, the Queen of Talk turned the tables on me, and helped me Show UP.

WHEN THE MASK GOT IN THE WAY

I also see the distinction between Showing Off and UP when I look at my experiences with acting. While acting was never my full-time career, I continued to enjoy it as a sideline. While I was on *Live at 5*, I got my fix in community theatre at a quaint little place called the Pond Playhouse. Then, before long, I started auditioning for small parts in TV and film. But you know what? I never fully committed to it. While I was secretly playing the role of a lifetime on *Live at 5*, convincing people I was one of the most confident people they knew, every time I walked into an audition I was focused on my inadequacy. I was focused on my fear. And I believe that's what most people do when they walk onto a stage or even into a cocktail party.

I loved my time in theatre, but I realize now that so much of it was really just Showing Off. I was putting on a character and going through the motions, instead of being in the moment and investing everything. This is pretense versus presence; pretending versus getting lost in the immediacy of performance. There are lots of actors out there who do the same, but it's the truly great ones whose work moves us profoundly—because they are so thoroughly stripped of their own mask. For me, it was more about layering another mask on top of my own.

When I worked on the film *Reversible Errors* (2004), I had the chance to do a scene with William H. Macy, who had become a household name after his Academy Award–nominated role in *Fargo*. I was cast as a reporter (as I so often was), and I interviewed Macy's character at the bottom of the steps of New Brunswick's Dorchester Penitentiary. He was absolutely lovely; down-to-earth, friendly, and supportive. Behind the scenes, the crew members (who invariably had the real beat on the actors) raved about how great he and his wife, Felicity Huffman, were. It was an exciting opportunity for me to work with "Bill" that day, but it wouldn't be the most memorable part of the experience.

In an unusual occurrence, I got a chance to chat with the director during a forced pause in the shooting schedule, and he made a point of telling me why I'd been chosen for my role. He said he'd learned long before that you can't hire regular actors to play reporters or anchors because they're just not convincing. Then he made a statement that felt like a warm, comforting blanket of recognition: "I bet most people in film don't give you credit for what a good actor you have to be to do your job day in and day out!" It was a balm for my insecurity about whether I was a "good enough" actor in the eyes of others. Although I never wanted my *Live at 5* audience to know how much acting was contributing to the Nancy-amalgam on screen, this feedback strangely fortified me.

In some ways, my most terrifying times were spent in the casting director's waiting room. It was a cauldron for the kind of well-hidden fear I harboured. I was always surrounded by other women who were roughly similar in appearance, and in my mind, vastly more experienced, more talented, and thereby more qualified for the job. The late John Dunsworth was, for a long time, the go-to casting director in Halifax. He later became famous for his role as Jim Lahey in *Trailer Park Boys*, but I first became acquainted with him in a small, well-lit casting room at the back of a little brick building on Barrington Street. I often wish I could go back to those days, peel off my cloak of fear, and allow my enthusiasm, passion, and talent to step into the spotlight. Lucky for me, John saw through the layers and discovered I had a spark.

Years later, after he had stepped away from the casting business, he was kind enough to do some private coaching with me before auditions. An unrelentingly generous guy, John wouldn't let me pay him, but he did sometimes accept donations for upcoming charity auctions he was hosting. He always told me he was there because he believed in me, and that meant so much. "All you need is a good director!" he would exclaim with his signature exuberance. He loved seeing the shift and growth as he coached me to erase the persona that was such a well-practiced part of me. Though he didn't use this term, I see now that he was trying to help me drop my mask.

I was lucky enough to have a good director when I was cast in a couple of outstanding plays at Halifax's Neptune Theatre. *Wit* and *Proof* were both Pulitzer Prize winners, and these gems marked my first professional roles on the stage. *Wit* was first, and it felt like I had been thrust into a high-end theatre school. I had a small role playing revolving characters but not very many lines—a safe way for me to start, and to study. I got to watch the creative evolution of Nicola Lipman's lead role and learned just how much it was a collaborative effort between actor and director.

Proof was my graduation into a more meaningful role. I played the sister of Catherine, the main character played by Carmen Grant. Once again, I was privileged to get to watch pure talent blossom on that stage. I learned so much from Carmen, but was also fortunate to have her as a mentor. In a twist of casting, this young theatre professional was the star, and I, the thirty-five-year-old TV celebrity, was the apprentice.

And the director never let me forget it.

He certainly didn't allow my local fame to soften his approach. In fact, he went overboard, treating me so far from "precious" it took my breath away. It may sound like I was thin-skinned, but other cast members regularly took me aside to tell me they thought I was doing well, and that they couldn't understand the director's seemingly hostile attitude toward me. Ever the people pleaser, I was working my ass off in rehearsal, but the director was determined in his disparagement of my efforts, picking away relentlessly at the way I delivered my lines, the way I walked, my expression when I was listening. It felt awful. And in retrospect, it was awesome. It tore me apart, but like every other hard thing in my life, it taught me how strong I was.

Looking back, I believe I understand what the director was trying to do. Like John Dunsworth, he was trying to get rid of my mask—which, admittedly, had to happen for me to give a good performance. However, he was going about it very differently than John had. He probably assumed my ego could take the beating, because of my projected confidence and public profile. That it would be good for me. He couldn't have understood the fragile impostor lurking underneath my ever-smiling exterior. I ended up more self-conscious than I'd been before, because I was so terrified to make a mistake.

In the end, I was proud to be part of this beautiful production and to be a member of the cast—which included William Christopher, who was famous for playing Father Mulcahy on one of my favourite TV shows of all time, M*A*S*H. In one episode of that classic show, the "Padre," as his friends call him, says, "I do believe people are essentially good." On that note, I do believe that tough director was trying to get the best out of me, and that my uncomfortable experience is now *proof* that I needed to start my excavation and begin to peel off my mask on my own. I hope I'll end up back on stage again someday, and I expect it will be a supremely different experience without my friend fear playing a starring role.

———————

Unfortunately, my fear, and the mask I've worn to hide it, have also interfered in my personal relationships. Not always overtly, but as a consistent underlying current. I was always so focused on what was wrong, it was hard to fully enjoy what was right. When GUS was standing guard, he prevented my imperfection from "getting out," but he also blocked *joy* from getting in. You know the old expression, "the more you put into it, the more you'll get out of it"? My dread of failure led me to believe that the less I put into it, the less I would risk. So, while my mask was all about success and achievement, beneath it I harboured a security blanket of *If I don't try my hardest and I fail, that's not really failure.* And that showed up in my love life.

I was a serial monogamist. Boyfriend after boyfriend. But the revolving door of suitors was not about conquest. It was *me* spinning, searching for unconditional love. I dated some truly lovely young men, but every time it didn't work out, I could chalk it up as further evidence that I was broken. I joked with my parents that I preferred the term *unclaimed blessing,* but I was secretly terrified of becoming an old maid. And society in those days amplified that pressure. When I'd go to a friend's wedding with a beau, the inevitable questions would be asked: *"So, when are you two getting married?"* My perfectionist translation: *"What's wrong with you that no man wants to marry you?"*

Eventually, a knight in shining armour rode into the picture on a thoroughbred horse. Actually, he was a handsome lawyer in an expensive suit, driving a Mercedes, but he was also supersmart, funny, and kind. Despite my best attempts to derail the relationship with jealousy and insecurity, he had staying power. Lo and behold, after a courtship, he proposed. Did I say "I do"? Damn right, I did. After a huge and fancy wedding we settled into married life, and over the next decade, we travelled, socialized, and had two of the sweetest boys who ever landed on this

Earth. Our life looked perfect from the outside, but as it turned out, I really was a little broken.

I was clinging to my mask. But I discovered that the more tightly I held onto it, the more cracks would appear. The more I kept my fear contained, the more it would find its way out in bursts of emotion—but only when I was out of public view. I would get frustrated with my kids, my husband, or, most often, myself. One of my sons unwittingly helped me understand this concept when he was very young. He had his own little mask. He didn't typically show a lot of emotion, but if he fell and hurt himself, it would all come pouring out. He could get a scrape on his knee and cry like his leg had been cut off. Slowly, I grasped that these small injuries were a doorway for his pain.

He went in for a day surgery when he was three. It all went as smoothly as we could have hoped. He had his teddy bear in his arms with a smile on his face when they put him to sleep, and that's the way he woke up. Happy and comfortable. Feeling the distinct relief of a mother whose toddler had just gone "under the knife," I took him home and thought that was the end of it. Two nights later, he had his first night terror. If you've never experienced the parenting *delight* of having a child go through this stage, count yourself lucky! Picture this: you wake up at midnight and your child is screaming and crying. You rush to their bedside. They seem to be wide awake, but are unable to hear you or register your calming words. All you can do is wait it out. It was terrifying. Mostly because I was worried about my kid, but also partly because, as a control freak, it threw me completely off balance. In hindsight, I see this chapter as a tough lesson in presence training. Try as we might, we couldn't wake our son up during these episodes, so we just had to hug him and wait it out. Sit with the pain. Embrace it.

Meanwhile, my own pain was persistent, but I hid it well. It was like a gnawing discomfort, an underlying anxiety that something wasn't right. I wasn't right.

Motherhood turned out to be yet another arena in which I could identify my shortcomings. It was like being a mom was built for guilt. If my kids didn't nurse well, that was my fault. If they didn't sleep through the night, my fault. If they got sick or hurt or sad, my fault. No one recognized this spiral because I hid it all behind my polished mask. But I knew in the deepest, truest part of myself, that my mask was suffocating me.

There have been many times in my life when others have shone a light on a path I didn't know was there. My friend Sandy did exactly that when I was taking my first tentative steps on this journey to authenticity. At the time, I would say I was intrigued by the "path" but not yet walking it. Sort of like staying in a hotel by the Camino de Santiago—watching TV, indulging in social media, downing little bottles of booze from the mini-fridge—all while keeping a curious eye on the spiritual pilgrims passing by. The Way, as it's called. *The way to where?* I wondered. I know the answer now: the way back to myself.

Sandy has done much for me over the years to show me a *way* I didn't know existed, but she has always resisted my referring to her as my teacher. For a time, I struggled to understand that, but I've finally come to appreciate that we all learn from each other. She didn't want to be placed on a pedestal, and neither do I. As the spiritual teacher, psychologist, and author Ram Dass said so succinctly, "We are all just walking each other home."

The first, and perhaps the greatest, gift Sandy gave me was a self-awareness of my mask. We were at a charity tea with a few other friends, gathered in a crowded space in a grand old Victorian house. It had long been a family home but was now a community gathering space—particularly for women. An auspicious location for this lesson to unfold. As the event was nearing its end, Sandy and I were standing in a small group when another friend suggested we extend our time together by doing something else afterwards. I think Sandy was the first to respond—an indication of her clarity at the time—and her words are seared into my soul.

"No thanks. My husband and I are really struggling in our marriage right now, so I feel like I just need to go home."

Talk about an invitation to presence! We were in our mid-thirties at the time, and this level of unadulterated dialogue was not typical of our relationship. Add to that, the fact that she was uttering these words in a normal tone of voice amidst a sea of women. An ocean of potential judgement. There was no sense of secrecy or discretion in her statement. The truth was, my marriage was suffering too, but I never would have felt the courage to utter those words. To air my failure in front of others so readily was unthinkable.

When I describe Sandy's openness as an invitation to presence, I mean she shocked me into the moment—her sheer honesty awakened my heart like a defibrillator. Standing there surrounded by upper-middle-class women in their full suits of armour—expensive dresses and shoes, hair done, makeup flawless—our masked surrogates of our selves, we were desperate to demonstrate how perfect our lives were.

I know this sounds like an elite group. So, *what*, you may ask, did we have to hide from? It's natural to assume that money is a gateway to ease. Not in my experience. Any worldly comfort only amplified my own internal discomfort. "What is *wrong* with me?!" was my silent refrain, standing at my bedroom window in the middle of the night, looking out at an idyllic scene. Watching the moon's reflection dance on the water, I reflected my own dis-ease back at myself. "Why can't I just be happy?" There's nothing quite like beating yourself up about beating yourself up to intensify a feedback loop of negativity.

> *The image of the moon*
> *ripples*
> *like the uncertainty in my soul*
>
> *I long for the stillness of*
> *my calm reflection*

It wasn't until years later, when I was immersed in a meditation at a yoga retreat, that I came to a sudden realization about that sad young woman by the window—and the reason for leaving that house, and the marriage that built it.

I was unlovable.

DARK

"These pains you feel are messengers. Listen to them."

—Rumi

I'm not a Buddhist, but many of the philosophies of the Buddha ring true for me, and the tenet that "life is suffering" was particularly helpful as I made my way into my existential exploration. I began to realize that when I went about my life feeling entitled, feeling that everything should be easy and carefree, I was constantly frustrated when things inevitably didn't go the way I wanted. On the other hand, when I started to change my mindset to accept that suffering is a part of life, it wasn't such a shock when things went awry. But here's the kicker: the Buddha—wise, enlightened being that he was—also taught that more often than not, we create our own suffering. And, like mould growing in a damp room, suffering will continue to fester until you do something about it. Avoiding it, or pretending it doesn't exist, will not solve the problem.

Here's my explanation of the difference between pain and suffering. I do not have a good relationship with the dentist. I don't blame my dentist—she's lovely—I blame my childhood experience.

It was before the days of youth-focused practices. There was no TV on the ceiling, no bucket of dollar-store toys as a reward, and no child-friendly bedside manner. For that matter, in my memory there wasn't much anesthetic either! A few years ago, I had to have a filling fixed. I was sitting in my dentist's chair, before any drilling had started, and I became conscious of how anxious I was. Here I was at fifty, about to have a simple procedure, and I was incredibly tense. Forget clenching my teeth, I was clenching my whole body. I took a deep breath as it dawned on me that this was a potent example of the distinction between pain and suffering. I was not in pain (not yet, anyway!) but in my fear I was *creating my own suffering.* I was allowing the anticipation of pain to cause me anguish.

The author and teacher Byron Katie puts it powerfully in a passage on her website:

> I discovered that when I believed my thoughts I suffered,
> but when I didn't believe them I didn't suffer, and that this
> is true for every human being. Freedom is as simple as that.
> I found that suffering is optional.

Suffering is optional. Let that sink in for a minute. (For more on Byron Katie, see page 248.)

Fear, baby...it's a sneaky little bastard. Did you know it's an acronym? *False Evidence Appearing Real.* I didn't come up with that, but I sure practiced it. For far too long, I allowed the past to cast a shadow on my present, but my path to self-understanding has led me to many surprising discoveries. Like the realization that I was *unlovable.*

It was quite a shock that day during a retreat when I came to a sudden awareness: *It wasn't his fault.* The "it" was my divorce from my first husband. This sense of knowing had instantly settled into my mind and my body, but this wasn't about blaming myself or doubting whether I was worthy of love. It was about being un-love-able. I wasn't *able* to be loved. Get ready for a cliché here… and I won't apologize for it, because clichés can also be universal truths. When I say I was un-love-able, I mean that I was not able to be loved by others *because I didn't believe I was worthy of love*. Truth was, I was not showing up as my whole self because there were too many parts of myself I didn't love.

Beginning this excavation work, delving into the deep dark hole I'd long been avoiding, helped me understand what was in it: fear, doubt, and insecurity. But I needed to go deeper in order to strip away the needless suffering in my life and to understand what lay beneath it. Once my dig had gotten me deep into the hole inhabited by my fear, I realized I needed to stop being afraid of the dark. I needed to embrace it.

EMBRACING THE DARKNESS

"What hurts you, blesses you. Darkness is your candle."
—Rumi

"You're an excellent faker."

Shortly before I left my television job at CTV, I was away on a girls' trip with two of my best friends. At a crossroads professionally, I didn't know what I was going to do next, but I knew that I had just been going through the motions for a long time. And while the thought of it scared me, I was intent on bringing authenticity into my work life. At a bar one evening, I had a conversation with a stranger that remains sharp in my mind even sixteen years later. A mutual friend had introduced us, and we were having a fun conversation. He was handsome and athletic, but it wasn't romantic—the boundaries were clear. All of a sudden, he spoke these words: "You're an excellent faker."

He was looking directly into my eyes, and through me. I was completely taken aback, and although I responded by trying to laugh it off, he was intent on challenging me. It may sound like he was mansplaining, but his words were delivered gently and sprang from pure intuition. He continued with a sense of curiosity: "I think the truth is that you're deeply unhappy, and you've got the world fooled into thinking you've got it all together." I felt in that instant like a mysterious force had knocked me into the present moment. I had been living in the past and the future, constantly focused on mistakes I'd already made and worrying about mistakes I might make in the future. He was right on so many levels. I was living the life I felt I was expected to live.

I realized, once I dug down, that I'd begun to feel like a mercenary in my role at *Live at 5*. I was staying for the paycheque, and I was feeling more disconnected from my true self by the day. But I also knew that to leave would be to swim against the current of public opinion. And I was right. When I actually got up the courage to quit, everyone thought I was crazy. Why would I leave a successful, high-profile job? Like any major decision in life, there was a kaleidoscope of reasons, but the greatest motivator was my need to move away from my mask.

Thankfully, some people did understand. I'll always treasure the phone call I got from one friend when he heard the news of my impending departure. "You're pulling a *Seinfeld*!" he exclaimed. I laughed and asked what he meant. "You're taking everyone by surprise by leaving when you're at the top of your game." That comment meant more to me than he ever knew.

Whenever I danced with others, clinging to my mask prevented me from engaging fully in the joy of movement and connection. And it didn't help that we were both usually dragging our past around the dance floor with us. "Baggage" is well named. It's like all our self-perceived flaws and resulting insecurities or doubts are packed into an overflowing suitcase. My take on this is that we all have a wounded child within us that we shield from the world. But without embracing that part of us and seeking to understand the hurt that exists there—without opening our luggage and taking a look at what's inside—we can't expand. We stay contracted. When we take those inner children into relationships with others, it gets complicated. We're desperate for our partner to take care of our wounded little selves but so reluctant to reveal them.

Along with our two sons, Geoff gave me another hugely meaningful gift. It was two years after our divorce, and we were both settled into new romantic relationships with partners who were secure enough to not be threatened by our co-parenting partnership. But I was still dragging some baggage around. Now packed tightly in there was a heavy new weight. *Guilt.* I can still picture where we were standing when Geoff issued a statement of reprieve that went straight to my heart. "Nance, you have got to take the guilt off your shoulders. I know I helped pile it on there, but it's time to let it go. I never would have left, but I see now that you did the right thing. And I'm glad you did." The character demonstrated by this gift of words explains why he remains to this day one of my best friends.

My second wedding was an entirely different affair than my first. Instead of a public production, it was private and intimate. Showing UP versus Showing Off. There were only ten people in our living room, including my fiancé, David, me, and my boys, and the full focus was on the vows we were making. There was no pomp or performance, but there was a party afterwards. We had gotten engaged at Christmas and invited those closest to us to celebrate with us early in the New Year, but we put one over on them. Our guests arrived at the "engagement party" to a *Just Married* sign, and our friend the judge in her robes! This new marriage was a fresh start, and I was convinced it was the remedy for my unhappiness. My new soulmate was going to, in the words of Jerry Maguire, "complete me."

Now, if this were a movie, at this point you might hear the music signalling impending doom. I'm pleased to report that no doom ensued. In fact, there was great celebration nine months later when our daughter burst onto the scene. But disappointment was around the corner, because I'd eventually realize that in spite of all the positive things in my life, I still had to face my *own* music.

———

In my experience, the concept of a soulmate sets the stakes pretty high. As the writer Anne Lamott puts it so brilliantly, "Expectations are resentments waiting to happen." You know that magical feeling of infatuation at the beginning of a relationship? I once heard a theory about this honeymoon phase that stopped me in my tracks. Consider this hypothesis: that new-love glow that makes you feel like you're walking on air has more to do with *you* than it does with the object of your affection. Loving what you see is as much about loving how you're seen.

Here's this seemingly perfect person perceiving all the best in you—and none of the worst. Eventually, though, reality settles in. You fell in love with each other's masks. It's really just another form of impostor syndrome: *I know I'm not as great as they think I am, but it sure feels good to be seen this way!* This may bear no resemblance to your experience, but I have lived this pattern more times than I care to reveal, and I can say beyond a shadow of a doubt that my mask and my fear got in the way of love.

we meet
our best selves
encounter each other
we love
what we see
through the other's eyes
until
we don't

perfect pairings
minus perfect
equals
dis pair
dissonance rules
resentment simmers
rising to a boil

but
like sand in an oyster
irritation challenges the soul
growing
pearls of wisdom

the choice is ours
stay closed and tight
more shadow than light

or
step out of our shells
and
open to love
our selves

It was a long time before I was ready to love myself. First, I had to take a look at what I loathed about myself. The late Louise Hay wrote in her book *You Can Heal Your Life* that everyone she'd ever met or worked with was suffering from some degree of self-loathing. And she made a simple but extremely compelling argument for changing that: "The more self-hatred and guilt we have, the less our lives work. The less self-hatred and guilt we have, the better our lives work, on all levels." Do you need more convincing than that to come along on this journey into the darkness? Just like an archaeological dig, this part is hard work, and often slow-going. It requires courage, determination, and resilience. And it is worth it.

OBSTACLES TO LOVE

"If we love ourselves in the wrong way, we become
incapable of loving anybody else. And indeed when
we love ourselves wrongly, we hate ourselves; if we
hate ourselves we cannot help hating others."
—Thomas Merton

Procrastination, for me, is all about fear. I start out being afraid I'm not up to the task. Then I feed my fear its favourite meal: *time,* which it devours. Avoidance of a task, event, or even a conversation is my protection against possible failure, because as I explained earlier, I know that if I don't really try, it's not really a failure. Then, just like when I was a kid, I wait until the deadline is breathing down my neck—until I'm going to get in trouble, or at least be revealed as the impostor I believe I am. The potential for disapproval is my rocket fuel.

Please notice that this is written in the present tense. And yes, the present *is* tense when I slide back into this pattern. It's one I recognize all too well, and unfortunately it triggers other patterns—sort of like dropping an Alka-Seltzer tablet in water. You remember the old jingle? "Plop, plop, fizz, fizz. Oh, what a relief it is!"—but this is the opposite of relief, because what come bubbling up to the surface are self-limiting beliefs: *I'm lazy. I can't do it. I'm not good enough.* And that not-enoughness is what I found in the dark depths of this pit.

I had been procrastinating getting rid of my mask, but it was time to do something about it. Before I could get real with others, though, I needed to get real, period. And part of that was admitting that I was in an abusive relationship...with myself. I had spent a lifetime looking for everyone else's approval, but it would never be enough because I didn't approve of myself. It was time for me to figure out why.

GETTING TO KNOW MY EGO

The way I see it, comparison and judgement—what I call "c&j"—are two of the most destructive forces in the world. They are the favoured instruments of ego—the part of our psyche that seeks to separate our self from others, and from ourselves. You can find lots of definitions for exactly what ego is, and I encourage you to engage in that worthy exploration, but for the purposes of sharing my journey with you, I'm going to offer my own perspective. When I'm looking out at the world, there's a part of me that is observing and judging what I see as right or wrong, good or bad, deserving or undeserving: that is my ego. I also turn that same demanding lens on myself.

My ego is a tricky little devil because he's a double agent. While he spends a lot of time assessing other people, situations, and relationships, he appears to be my advocate. Like a boxer's coach, he stands in my corner, wiping my brow and building me up with running commentary: *"He's not as smart as you"*; *"She's not as talented as you"*; *"You're the best!"* But when the bell rings and I step back into the ring, there he is again. Except now he's my opponent, taking swings at me and trying to knock me down. Trash talk is his specialty: *"You don't have what it takes"*; *"You're such a loser"*; *"Give up, Stupid."* Ah, the re-emergence of GUS. My ego is like GUS's mentor. Although they have some overlap in their outlook, my ego is more sophisticated and he's concerned not just with my safety, but the larger issue of my identity.

You see, over time, my ego becomes a castle, built all around me. The walls are my identity, and the stones that form it are stories about who I am, what I have done, and what's been done to me. The higher and thicker the walls are, the more I'm trapped inside and the less connected I am to others. And when I am alone in this castle, all I can hear are my own thoughts echoing back to me. Patrolling the perimeter of my castle is GUS, the fearful flunky whose full-time job it is to keep me safe. But here's the irony: the more my castle is fortified, the weaker I am. Like any fortification, it's a defensive system. All about protection and projection. As spiritual teacher Eckhart Tolle puts it, "the ego creates separation, and separation creates suffering." Hiding inside the walls of ego, I am in darkness.

Let's talk about *your* identity for a moment. What's your answer if I ask, "Who are you?" Chances are your first response includes a role—a function you perform (I'm a teacher. I'm a sales rep. I'm a presentation coach). If I ask you to go beyond that and I pose the question again, you might respond with a relational identity. In my case, I'm a mother of three. I'm one of six kids. I'm David's wife. But that's still not who I *am*. And your roles are not who *you* are. They just represent who you are *in relation to others*. These roles of mine are of huge importance to me, but there was a me before my kids came along, before I was married, before I had a job, and that's what I'm driving at.

So, I ask again: Who are you?

It's hard to find an answer, isn't it? The first time I did this exercise, I tried every angle to define myself: jobs, geography, gender, age, personality traits, appearance, even family history. But it was all just a story. The story of my life. None of it is who I *am*.

It was my choice to leave *Live at 5* when I did, and it was the right timing, but it wasn't easy. It was the only job I'd ever held as an adult, and partly because of the high profile, I had come to be defined by it. By others and by myself. Walking away was a bit like being pulled out of the Earth's atmosphere. Feeling untethered, I thought about putting *Has-been* on my business card under my name but decided too many people might take me seriously. Who was I if I wasn't a TV host? It might have been a challenge, but it was a healthy one. It led me to a more authentic path—a long and twisty one, but a path just the same. It set me on a trajectory away from my mask, and away from Showing Off.

COMPARISON & JUDGEMENT

"Comparison is the thief of joy."
—Theodore Roosevelt

I remember listening to a van-load of twelve-year-old girls chatting away one day. I'm sure I'm not the first "chauffeur" in the world to discover that if you're strategically quiet, you can foster a situation that's ripe for gaining "intelligence." Once the chatter winds up, they forget the vehicle is being actually being driven by Momentum. As I listened in silence, I could hear a pattern of oneupmanship emerging. A jockeying for social status. *Who knows who? Who's done what? Who's gone where? Who wears what?* It was all about comparison and judgement (c&j), and it made me wish I could put the brakes on this sense of competition. I found it disturbing at first, and then I recognized it as a *pack practice* as old as the human species. At their age, these girls were just getting warmed up.

In the land of c&j there must be winners and losers, and that means we're all either one or the other. I remember clearly falling into this same trap when I was young. I loved art but wasn't as creative as my best friend, the daughter of an accomplished artist. I did well in school but wasn't as smart at the aforementioned Shelley H, whose mother was a teacher. I liked sports, but I was never the first one chosen for teams. Even by the time I was ten years old, I was leaving behind my carefree tomboy self and felt caught in this vortex of comparison.

I know now that my ego is what makes me any of the following: offended, embarrassed, resentful, frustrated, judgmental, defensive, inferior, superior, jealous—the list could go on all day. These are the masks my fear and ego wear. My ego loves resistance; it gives him something to chew on. But it's not all negative. As a boxing coach, he's also a promoter and concerned about my "brand." He's always looking for ways to enhance it by associating me with success—even the success of others.

Our kids are often proxies for approval. My oldest son was gifted with the love of singing and perfect pitch from the time he was a toddler. As he grew, I loved seeing his passion blossom and got true enjoyment out of it. I was proud of him—but let me unpack this statement. My pride was definitely rooted in love for the sweet little boy brave enough in grade four to step in front of his whole school to sing Leonard Cohen's "Hallelujah." He performed it flawlessly, with sensitivity and musicality, and the audience was floored—particularly the other parents in the room. This was a milestone for Andrew, and as it turned out, the start of a musical path that would lead him to Berklee College of Music in Boston. But it was also the beginning of a vicarious pleasure I gained from his praise and popularity.

When he started to post covers on YouTube at fourteen as Andrew M (his last name is Machum), he moved into a bigger pond, but the online world was impressed by this small frog! His cover of Bruno Mars's "Grenade" got amazing traction and the views steadily climbed. And so, it started. I loved sharing my son's musical successes on Facebook and seeing friends share them as well, but I also noticed when they didn't. I would make a mental note: *Oh, there's jealousy there.* But I was experiencing the flip side of envy: the spotlight that shone on my son was lighting me up again.

People would often rave to me, "Oh you must be bursting with pride," and I was quick to be self-deprecating, pointing out that Andrew clearly had not inherited his singing voice from me (though I'm pretty certain I was a great singer in a previous life because of how much I love it!). I would always follow that humility with the credit he was due: "What I'm proud of is his work ethic, and his courage to put himself out there." That was true. What was also true was that my pride in his talent existed in both healthy and unhealthy ways. It *is* the first of the seven deadly sins after all!

The most fertile breeding ground for c&j in our time is social media—*Like, Don't Like, Love*—it's a funhouse of comparison and judgement. Oh, but the ego can be easily bruised by the barrage of others' successes. Because of its natural scarcity mentality, ego doesn't grasp the concept that "a high tide floats all boats." Instead, it thinks, *What* you *have makes me less-than—so if I bring you down, I won't be so low by comparison.* This means we have a planet full of people who are, at least publicly, content to share their happiness but desperate to hide their despair.

As I've said to my kids many times, social media can be dangerous for our mental health because it's so easy to fall into the trap of comparing our inner life to everyone else's outer life—our reality with their personal branding. In other words, our Showing UP to their Showing Off. And it's a platform that's built for Showing Off. It promises connection, but all too often delivers amplified isolation.

Ego despises the judgement of others. Unless it's approval or praise, it's not welcome. It's appropriate to me that judgement starts with a J. I've learned to see this letter as a hook that catches any criticism that swims by. My cheek bears the symbolic scar of having allowed these external judgements to steer my life for too long. But I couldn't stop obsessing about the judgement of others until I found a way to stop judging myself. And to do this, I had to look at the stories I'd been telling myself *about* myself, those stones that had built my castle.

STORYTELLING

In presentation, storytelling plays a crucial and pivotal role in creating a relationship with an audience. The oldest form of communication, it connects the two hemispheres of the brain and helps us understand new concepts. It also connects us to each other as human beings. Stories allow us to see our own pain or joy reflected in the experiences of others. Personally, I believe in an even deeper value of story: it has the ability to connect us to ourselves. As valuable a tool as story is, it's the journey toward taking control of our own personal narrative that powers our ultimate self-awareness.

Before I could make sense of myself, I needed to make sense of my journey. What were the lessons—both painful and joyful—that had brought me to this moment, this version of myself? Like computer software, we can get slow and clunky before an upgrade, but a paradigm shift occurs when we download new information. I know now that I am not the plot of the would-be movie of my life, but I couldn't fully comprehend that until I was willing to process it all. I needed to take all my data—successes, failures, betrayals, loves, fears, stumbles, hurts, scars, joys, celebrations, and losses—and run them through a sophisticated yet simple program to find meaning. My meaning. *What do I mean?* Only then could I move forward into *Why do I matter?* Of course, this journey is not as straightforward and clinical as inputting data, it's far messier than that, but when I am willing to do the work to find a way out of this darkness, something inevitably *clicks*.

Like scaffolding, my story provided a structure as I embarked on the darkest phases of my dig. The faces I saw along the way had all contributed to who I'd become. Even if they had taken something away from me, even if I viewed them as villains, they inarguably contributed to my narrative. But they were not who I was, and neither was my story. To use a phrase that is usually framed as an insult, it was a *self-centred* endeavour—but, as I've learned first-hand, centring myself is good for everyone around me. It's the same principle as the flight attendant's instructions to put on your own oxygen mask first. I discovered that the more I grounded myself in my own journey, the more I could breathe.

JEALOUSY

Jealousy is an example of a destructive pattern that disrupted my relationships through the years (even with friends in childhood) and it's not hard to understand why. It's known as the "green-eyed monster" for a reason, but the most powerful and succinct analysis I've ever heard of jealousy is found in a quote from B. C. Forbes, the Scottish-American financial journalist who founded *Forbes* magazine: "Jealousy is an inner consciousness of one's own inferiority. It is a mental cancer."

I realize now it was just another form of impostor syndrome. *I know I'm not really as great as they think I am,*. Jealousy was the manifestation of that facade being threatened. Being around others who made me feel less-than was like picking a scab off my deepest wound. I can think of many boyfriends (and two husbands) who bore the brunt of this manifestation of my insecurity. As I learned through experience, it is an obstacle to love.

It's not surprising that someone who doesn't feel their own value would be on constant alert for their partner finding others attractive. This is why it was an outgrowth of c&j: my ego saw other women as a potential hazard. While I was focusing on my deficits, I was threatened by their assets! In fact, I believe this kind of threat triggers the reptilian brain—because one of those survival instincts is to procreate. For me, though, I think it was also connected to actual survival. My excavation of my own darkness helped me acknowledge that beneath this destructive emotion was a deep-seated fear of abandonment.

For the first chapter of my life, Laura was my best friend. In a way, she was my first love. It was purely platonic, but I worshipped her, and fancied her as the Diana Barry to my Anne Shirley. We did a lot of growing together. We played endlessly, building forts on both our properties—needing only fallen pine needles to create the impression of walls, and our imaginations to construct the rest. We'd stay outside all day, jumping the stream that ran between our yards to traverse the distance between our houses. We laughed a lot, but there were also occasional fights, and I've always remembered one with regret.

We had just had a yard sale at the bottom or my long driveway, raising money for a kids' charity called Rainbow Haven. A disagreement had sprung up early on when we tussled over whose driveway we'd plant ourselves in. I won that skirmish when I pointed out that hers was mid-hill and mine opened up at the roadside into a natural area from which to sell our "goods." Did I mention I was bossy? My control issues started early! Laura tempered that idiosyncrasy and navigated my need for control with her easy personality—but she was no pushover!

The real problem developed when another girl got involved. She was a friend of Laura's who went to a different school, and I felt my first pangs of jealousy because of her relationship with *my* best friend. When a dispute arose about who would keep the money until our heroic delivery to the charity, the other girl sided with Laura—leaving me feeling excluded; a fate worse than death to a ten-year-old.

As an adult, I can see the anger that sparked from me that day for what it truly was: jealousy and fear of abandonment. But at the time, I just felt hurt and mad. So mad that I stomped up the hill back home. You'd think the sheer exertion might've settled me down...but no. I marched up to my room in tears. And when my room could no longer hold my agitated energy, I stormed out to the small deck off my parents' bedroom. I yelled down at the top of my lungs to Laura and the interloper that we were no longer friends. We were done!

Of course, within a week we were reconciled, but life eventually took us in different directions. It wasn't until I learned Laura was terminally ill with lung cancer several years ago that I made the effort to reconnect. I'll always regret the decades we lost.

Across all those years, I can still tune in to the old reverberations attached to my resentment of that other girl and the burning jealousy I felt. I know this experience was not where my fear of abandonment began, but digging into those feelings helps me understand a lifelong pattern, and forgive the child inside myself who still harbours the insecurities.

MEETING MY SHADOW

"People will do anything, no matter how absurd, in order to avoid facing their own souls. One does not become enlightened by imagining figures of light, but by making the darkness conscious."
—Carl Jung, *Psychology and Alchemy*

I had learned a little about Carl Jung's concept of the "shadow" in an introductory psychology course at university, and I remember being intrigued by his definition of this dark side of our personality. He described it as "the person you would rather not be." I wasn't ready to face my own shadow then, but the subject matter resonated. I *was* ready twenty years later when the theory was introduced to me in a more intimate way by author Debbie Ford in *The Dark Side of the Light Chasers*. It was one of those books that mystically appeared at just the right moment.

I knew there was a lot I didn't like about myself, and Ford's work helped me accept that as a normal part of being human. When I read her reference to the masks we wear in an effort to hide those parts of ourselves, I knew I was on the right track. I had already identified and begun the work of disengaging my mask, so I felt like she was speaking directly to me.

It turns out the things that drive us crazy about others are a reflection of the characteristics we do not want to admit to in ourselves, or as Jung put it, "Everything that irritates us about others can lead us to an understanding of ourselves." The first time I heard that idea, I resisted it. Thinking about the people in my life by whom I felt triggered, my immediate response was, "Nope. Not me!" Of course, that was ego and fear responding. When I think about it in retrospect, I can see GUS guarding the gates to his lair, attempting to keep me from exploring this terrain any further. As much as it initially seemed impossible, it was *spot-on*. Although it took a while to understand and accept the concept, the truth was like a boomerang. I had managed to duck the first time it flew by, but eventually it came back 'round and hit me square in the heart.

I once worked with someone who could best be described as a big bundle of negative energy. He put on a great show when the lights and camera came on, but behind the scenes he seemed deeply unhappy. Who else would, after having a warm conversation with one of his "superiors" in a communal work area, say something disparaging about them the moment they walked away? The first time this happened, I did a double-take. *Did he mean to say that out loud?* Unfortunately, what was startling at first became commonplace and it poisoned our workplace. But now I am grateful to that co-worker for having been my teacher. Ensconced in unhappiness, putting on a daily show, I know he shone a light on a part of my own shadow, and showed me how I didn't want to be. Furthermore, he helped me realize that my mask was designed to hide my own discontent and control others' perceptions of me.

One line in particular from Debbie Ford's book hit home for me: "It's not enough to say 'I know I am controlling.' We must see what controlling has to teach us." For a long time, control was my life preserver. It's what I clung to in order to prevent myself from drowning in my own fear. And I was particularly touchy about anyone pointing it out. What lives in the shadow dwells in the dark for a reason. It doesn't want to be seen, so it takes determination and persistence to bring it to light. I had to dig into all the ways control was surfacing in my life before I could uncover its source.

Sometimes on this quest, I got lucky with two-for-one deals. Here's an example. My husband has a tendency to be late for things. Early in our relationship, when I was still wearing the rose-coloured glasses of new love, I came to a generous conclusion. I decided that—although it was a frustrating habit—his tardiness was directly connected to his optimism. He's a blue-sky thinker, and that's been a vital advantage to him as an entrepreneur. He sees possibility where others don't, which is a pretty charming trait. However, he also thinks he can tick twenty items off his to-do list in ten minutes, and the resulting tardiness began to annoy me. It became a source of friction in our relationship, and

I came to the conclusion that both of our shadows were showing up in this pattern: I hated feeling out of control, and he hated being controlled.

So, there I was in 2012, a forty-six-year-old in a perimenopausal spiral, struggling with a hormone-induced emotional roller coaster. On this particular day, I'm running late for an appointment and frantically searching for my keys. My frustration is amping up by the second, and the fuel on this fire is my self-loathing. Suddenly, David, who has been witnessing this tornado of destructive energy, jolts me out of my spin by yelling at me—loudly: "Nancy!" Having captured my attention, he continues emphatically: "You're disorganized! Accept it and get over it! It doesn't make you a bad person!" If you've ever watched *Seinfeld*, you know Elaine has a habit of physically pushing people—accompanied by a "Get *out!*"—when she's surprised. That's how I felt when David yelled at me that day. Like I had been knocked over by his words. But what actually sent me reeling was the sudden realization that I *did* think being disorganized made me a bad person.

There were moments when digging that I hit the jackpot, and this was one of them. Here's why: My husband's startling statement had immediately connected to another concept I had learned recently. That my inner critic—that little bastard who was always nattering away, picking at all my psychological scabs—was saying things I'd actually heard before. I began to realize then that the voice in my head was equipped with a script, the lines of which have been written by others; people in my life who have criticized me (sometimes unrelentingly) and made me feel less-than. Standing there in the kitchen that day, I was transported back to grade 4.

Mrs. W did not succumb to my charisma. Perhaps she couldn't see me through the pile of papers on my desk. I wouldn't realize until I was an adult that I had lived my whole life with ADHD, but looking back, I now recognize that my grade 4 teacher tried to tell me. She did not do so, however, with a terrific bedside manner. One day, hovering over my desk, she made the pronouncement: "Nancy Regan, you are the most disorganized child I have ever seen in my life!" This would have been hurtful if she had said it to me privately, but Mrs. W expressed this opinion loudly, in front of the entire class, and that triggered something within me.

You know the moment from Lucy Maud Montgomery's *Anne of Green Gables* when Anne Shirley is so incensed at Gilbert for calling her red braids "carrots" that she breaks a slate over his head? Well, in my own moment of humiliation, I felt that same sense of indignation and rage. It's just as well I didn't have a slate handy! Instead of allowing this overwhelming energy within me to translate into violence, I let it move me. In a reaction that went against everything I'd been taught, I looked this teacher straight in the eye, stood up, and walked out of the classroom. Once in the hallway, I calmly plucked my jacket off its hook, put it on, and walked out the front door of the school—and then ran like hell the half-kilometre home. I remember to this day the feeling of my heart racing, and how I'd periodically cast a glance over my shoulder for fear I was being chased by Mrs. W or the principal.

Since I sometimes had lunchtime piano lessons in our basement, my mother greeted my early arrival with only a small measure of surprise, but she quickly realized that wasn't the reason for my untimely appearance. Upon hearing my tale of woe, Mom was not altogether without compassion but insisted I return to school for the afternoon. *Gulp.* That was tough. But I did it. To my pleasant surprise, I was welcomed back into the fold by my class-mates with a sense of awe and delight. I had apparently caused quite a scene when I departed, leaving poor Mrs. W flabbergasted and uncharacteristically speechless. When I think about it now, I understand why. She had been wielding her power in an irrespon-sible and damaging manner, and my walking out was a simple but profoundly effective way of taking away that power.

Before I returned to class, I had to visit with the school princi-pal in the library. I have never forgotten that meeting. Elsie Parker was the antithesis of Mrs. W—a truly loving presence; an educator whose strength came not through fear and loathing, but a rare gen-tle power she wielded wisely. We had always gotten along famously. So, there we were: Mrs. Parker perched on the edge of the librarian's desk and me standing before her, ready to face the music. But what she said took me by surprise. "Nancy, dear, I think you just let your anger get the best of you." Gratified, I eagerly nodded in response to her assessment. Because I was unfamiliar with the expression, I was convinced she was telling me I had done the right thing. *The best of you*—that had to be good, right? Maybe that's why, when she told me I'd have to apologize, I readily agreed. I have always been adept at reading other people's energy, and in that moment, I could sense Mrs. Parker's reluctant respect for the way in which I had stood up for myself. I'm also certain that her professional demeanour belied a desire to break into laughter at the hilarity of it all. I'm proud to say that for the rest of the school year, Mrs. W never treated me, or anyone else, like that again.

I've always had a strong barometer for justice. Often, I've found myself jumping to the defence of someone I felt was being unfairly treated. Whether I know them or not, if someone is being picked on or cheated, my instinct is to protect. This is in direct opposition to my natural aversion to conflict. It's also ironic given I've spent a lifetime bullying myself. This little story is my first memory of not only standing up for myself, but also allowing my inner wisdom to take the lead. In that moment, I forgot all about Showing Off and Showed UP!

However, even though I felt supported by the principal, it turned out Mrs. W's words had landed somewhere deep inside me that day—and taken root. And the energy with which they were delivered served as fertilizer for my burgeoning concern that I was flawed. I don't typically enjoy being yelled at, but when David shouted at me that day, he shocked me into consciously recognizing a shame I had carried for years.

So, what prevents us from contemplating the crap that keeps us trapped in fear? For me, the answer is found in just that one word: *shame*. Many people spend their whole lives hiding from their own darkness. But until you turn and face it, and find a way to sit with it, you can't step out of the fear. And in my experience, you can't do that until you take a long hard look at shame.

SHAME

"Shame is the intensely painful feeling or experience of believing that we are flawed and therefore unworthy of love and belonging."
—Brené Brown, *The Gifts of Imperfection*

My seeds of fear
were planted
in the fertile soil
of shame

The wounds are weeds
with stubborn roots
I cannot speak their name

They're strangling
the flowers
in the garden of
my heart
but I make light
of my hurt
because I'm terrified
of the dark

I am a thumb-sucker. No past-tense here. Because, like an alcoholic, although I no longer indulge in the habit, I believe I still harbour the addiction. This self-soothing caused me deep shame as a kid. As I grew, I got the message that it was no longer acceptable. But I couldn't stop. I didn't *want* to stop. I would curl up and pop my thumb in my mouth, and my nervous system shifted gears from chaos to comfort. I was dependent on that feeling. But by the time I started school, I had received the message loud and clear from parents, siblings, babysitters, and even friends: only babies suck their thumbs.

When you're five or six and desperate to be a big girl, "baby" is a loaded word, an insult extraordinaire, so I did what many addicts do: I let shame drive my habit underground. I hid it. I was no less needy of my comfort fix, so I'd sneak off in the daytime and hibernate in my closet. By then, my tattered pink blankie had been reduced to a tiny corner of satin, so I learned to find other soft surrogates. My mother's fur coat only came out of the hall closet on very special occasions, so it was a ready and steady companion. By the time I was ten, though, I felt the shame deeply. I knew there was something wrong with me because I would rather have been caught dead than caught sucking my thumb. I could only do it under the cover of darkness, safe in my bed. It wasn't until I went to camp at the age of twelve that I finally broke the habit. I was in a cabin with eleven other preteen girls, and the possibility of discovery made me quit cold turkey. This is just another example of the way small insecurities can become lifelong scars, and leave us with a cumulative feeling of ever-deepening shame.

Perhaps no one is more well-versed in shame than Brené Brown. The now bestselling writer and speaker had no idea she was going to take the world by storm when she showed up on stage at a 2010 TEDX conference in her hometown of Houston, Texas. She also didn't know that this presentation, *The power of vulnerability*, would end up being one of the most watched videos on the internet (it currently has over 55 million views). A researcher in the field of social work, she started out by sharing a finding that had fundamentally changed her. She went on to talk about connection as a fundamental human need—"why we're all here"—and her career's worth of evidence that in order to have authentic connection, we need to allow ourselves to *be authentic*.

That may sound simplistic at first blush, but I was committed to becoming more myself, so I was immediately tuned in to her message. Then she hit me with a sucker punch. She had discovered that the number-one thing that prevents people from being authentic and enjoying real and rewarding connection with others...is shame. This revelation rocked me. I knew I was flawed, but I had never contemplated how my insecurities were preventing me from being vulnerable, or allowing myself to be seen by others.

That there was "courage" in being yourself, "whole-heartedly," imperfections and all. This had long been a challenge I'd faced in romantic relationships, in friendships, even with family members. Authenticity was something I could wave a flag about, but shame was literally nothing to be proud of. And Brené had boiled it all down to an enduring feeling of not being "enough." Bingo! That, I could relate to. I began to dig down into my own shameful depths, to see what I'd find.

My lack of organizational ability, as called out by Ms. W, was far from my only sense of inadequacy; it was part of a bigger deficit—a boulder in the dark shadows that I had spent a lifetime trying to hide. I wasn't officially diagnosed with Attention Deficit Hyperactivity Disorder (ADHD) until I was fifty years old, so for most of my life, my distinct inability to focus for any period of time just felt like more evidence of my not-enoughness. Whenever I tried to listen to a speaker, or read material I found less than riveting, my mind would wander—playing on my mental monkey bars and then swinging back 'round to berate me for my inattention. But then I read an article by Noelle Faulkner in the *Guardian* called "The Lost Girls: 'Chaotic and curious, women with ADHD all have missed red flags that haunt us.'" I'll tell you this: I didn't have any trouble concentrating on this content.

The premise of the piece was that a whole generation of girls, like me, missed out on diagnoses because almost all ADHD studies had been done on boys. Furthermore, although this condition may often manifest as disruptive behaviour in boys, "it can also make little girls feel like they'll never be good enough." Check! And then this powerful statement from the author: "There are many women like me: 'lost girls', so we've been called. Chaotic and curious, sometimes we feel like superheroes; other times, super-failures." Check! Check! Whenever someone else's words resonate like this did, it feels like the author has peered inside my mind. I'm not sure I would have ever been diagnosed with ADHD as a kid, because I worked too hard to mask my deficits. And having done a lot more research now, I know it's typical for girls to internalize their frustration while boys are much more likely to act it out.

———

Henry Ward Beecher said, "Every man should keep a fair-sized cemetery in which to bury the faults of his friends." I wish I'd had a plot to bury my own. Instead, I buried my strengths, achievements, and successes, and put my flaws up on a pedestal. It was like a version of the "confirmation bias" scientists are warned to be wary of. I was always looking for evidence to support my hypothesis that I was not enough. My enduring self-assessment, and the secret I never wanted anyone to know, was that I was a dork. Unconsciously, I kept a running tally of all the things that were wrong with me: pigeon-toed feet, overbite, the curvature in my lower back that made my bum stick out, and the enduring assessment that I talked too much. I started to copy others in an effort to seem cooler. For instance, my older sister had beautiful penmanship, so I tried to imitate it. Decades later, I still sometimes mistake my writing for hers.

But my inadequacy wasn't all in my mind. As I grew, my physical body became part of the problem. Yes, like many other women, I had body issues. When I was thirteen and surrounded by girls sprouting breasts, I became alarmed that mine had yet to make an appearance. I can't help but chuckle now, thinking of Laura and I attempting to take matters into our own hands. "We must, we must, we must increase our bust!" we'd chant as we thrust our arms forward and back, praying fervently that this ritual would result in the desired growth. I've never forgotten the strange mixture of amusement and dismay we experienced when Laura's mom, Ineke (a Dutch artist), told us we wouldn't need bras until we could put a pencil under our boobs without it falling!

As it turned out, my butt didn't need such encouragement. It expanded to a point that, as a teenager, I felt obliged to wrap a towel around my waist when I walked down the beach (though I'd love to have that ass now!). I learned early that if I nestled into the sand, I could bury my excess bum sufficiently so that my flat stomach could take centre stage. I was eternally grateful to the genius who "supported" flat-chested girls like me and introduced the padded bikini top.

It's hard for me to imagine now how I ever took part in those horrid pageant swimsuit competitions. The Miss Nova Scotia one was bad enough. I was painfully self-conscious. Just take a moment and consider this: you're paraded in front of a crowd, every member of which is perusing your physique and judging how it stacks up against all the others. A friend of mine refers to it now as a "cattle call." Perhaps the worst thing about winning that "title" was that it meant I'd then have to strut my bathing suit–clad self down a runway in Toronto. On national television.

Preparing for the Miss Canada debacle was the closest I've ever come to an eating disorder. I was obsessed with shrinking. Determined to slim my bottom half to more closely match my top. Dieting and working out with a firm focus on needing to be firmer. The thought of showing my cellulite to the world made me want to throw up—and it's just as well that I could never make myself vomit, because my mindset at the time was primed for bulimia. While some friends were concerned I was getting too skinny, all

I could see when I looked in the mirror were the obvious spots where my skin was plump and dimpled instead of smooth and tight. Today I know this psychological state is called body dysmorphia, and I wish I could tell you I grew out of the habit of battling my own body in my twenties. Or in my thirties. Or in my forties... What can I say, I'm a slow learner. But at least I'm in good company.

Far too many of us have an adversarial relationship with our own bodies. In the ground-breaking book *The Beauty Myth*, author Naomi Wolf argues that beauty is the "last, best belief system that keeps male dominance intact." Here's the equation I bought into for too long: Beauty = approval = love. It took me decades to discover I had it backwards, and it had to start from within. *Love = approval = beauty.* But in order to begin that journey, I had to dig even further into my shame to hit that rock at the bottom of the hole: trauma.

TRAUMA

"Anything that is wrong with you began as a survival mechanism in childhood.
—Dr. Gabor Maté

I used to think of trauma exclusively in terms of violence, abuse, bullying, racist attacks, or natural disaster—things that happen *to* you. But Dr. Gabor Maté, an addictions expert who specializes in the treatment of trauma, makes this distinction: "Trauma is what happens inside you as a result of these traumatic events." He also asserts that all addiction can be linked to childhood trauma, and that among the lasting ramifications of this trauma, we disconnect from our emotions and our body, we find it difficult to be in the present moment, and we learn to look at the world and ourself through a negative lens. Oh, and we tend to be defensive toward other people! (I checked a lot of those boxes.) I became an adult who was hypersensitive to criticism from family, from friends and boyfriends, and eventually from work. A thin-shelled egg is easily cracked. It's said that "you can't find yourself at the bottom of a bottle," but that may be exactly what addicts are looking for—lost parts of themselves. In the documentary *The Wisdom of Trauma*, Maté outlines two fundamental needs of early childhood: attachment to caregivers, and authenticity. That second one—"connection to ourselves"—gets disrupted when the world tells us to *suppress who we really are*.

For most of us, that suppression first occurred in our family of origin, and that was true for me. I was the fourth-oldest child in my family, but I was not the first fourth child. A brother, John, whom I never got a chance to know, died before I was born. In those days, as I see it, grief was customarily buried with the dead—particularly when it was a loss as painful as that of a young child. Society didn't make space for grieving as a process, and when you had three other young children, as my parents did, life didn't make room for it either. But my family had suffered this huge blow before my arrival, and as I grew up, it affected me too. I see that now. Something that Maté says in the documentary puts it all in perspective: "Children don't get traumatized because they're hurt. They get traumatized because they were alone in their hurt."

I hadn't been around for the trauma of John's death, but I felt the aftershocks. Though I didn't realize it at the time, I grew up with an impending sense of the fragility of life—that you can be there one day and gone the next. Decades later, that would surface when my own children were babies. As a mom, fear was my constant companion. It became something my kids joked about as they got older. "Don't mind Mom," they'd say to friends as my neuroses surfaced when we were out on the water. "We're pretty sure her whole family died in a boating accident in a previous life!" But beneath my fear was a deep, unacknowledged pain.

the greatest loss of my life
happened before I was born
his departure
shadowed my arrival
I wish I could've broken my brother's fall.

In a way, I believe I grew in grief—I'm talking womb-level development. But I think it goes even further than that. The growing field of epigenetics, which studies how our behaviours and environments can actually change the way our genes express, has shown that grief can be intergenerational. Trauma unhealed can be inherited.

I never met my paternal grandmother because she died before I was born, but she suffered what would probably be diagnosed today as serious depression when her seven-year-old daughter died following a simple surgery. The saying "She was never the same" echoes in my head. As I've navigated what felt like more than my fair share of loss and grief in the past fifteen years, I've often thought of her. Her name was Rose, and I'll tell you more about her later. The grandmother I did know was Marg, and she may well have handed down some abandonment issues. When I interviewed her for a legacy video at the age of ninety-four, she marvelled aloud that her parents had sent her away to a boarding school at the tender age of five. "Can you imagine that?" she asked.

I believe that when I arrived on the planet, I felt the unspoken grief that existed because of the death of my would-have-been brother. I was a joyful toddler who had been nicknamed *Fancy Nancy* because of my natural exuberance, but the empath in me perceived an energetic void and assumed I was supposed to fill it. It was bigger than me, so I tried to be bigger, louder, funnier, better. I started Showing Off. As an adult, I've always had a habit of filling silence in a group in order to make other people feel comfortable. Between the political gene and my TV training, I've had a lot of practice. My husband refers to it as my "talk-show-host instinct"—always wanting the conversation to be smooth and effortless, and feeling the need to guide it back there when it goes off course.

But this habit of mine is more than a leftover from TV—it's a legacy from my childhood. My driven desire to make it all okay. That same default setting is a huge part of the reason I've always leaned away from friction. As a young empath, I felt discord deeply when others fought or got in trouble, and I decided to steer clear of conflict—for life! Looking back over the years now, I recognize a pattern of holding resentments close to my heart rather than speaking them. This was intended to save everybody involved—including me—the pain of picking the scab. *But scabs turn into scars.*

My perception of life as precarious was strangely solidified by politics. I was twelve when my father lost his job in 1978. That was over four decades ago, but when I close my eyes I can take myself right back to one particular moment from that election night. He had been premier since I was four years old, so this was the only occupation I had ever known my dad to have. At my tender age, it felt like a powerful blow when the people of Nova Scotia very publicly fired him. This pivotal juncture in his career path was also a powerful moment for me. I had already learned the importance of people liking you, but this experience taught me that the approval and acceptance of others could make or break you. That night, the rejection broke me. I remember distinctly my decision not to go to campaign headquarters with the rest of the family. I certainly didn't let on that I was upset, and my reaction was not a reflection of my parents'. Although I'm sure they were disappointed, I remember them being calm, cool, and collected. Not me. As I sat alone in our TV room and watched the rest of my family standing on stage with my father as he conceded defeat, I bawled my eyes out. Even now as I write these words, a lump forms in my throat. Not because I'm still upset about it, but rather because to me, this is a physical reminder that I still have some work to do in processing the feelings of that inner child of mine.

But I'm getting ahead of myself; we're not done with the dark yet.

SHAME AS A TOOL

Shame has been weaponized for centuries. And no one has done it better than organized religions. Of course, parents can wield this double-edged sword powerfully as well—as can family members, teachers, friends, and enemies. If I make you feel ashamed, afraid, unworthy, I can control you. I can't think of a realm in which this has been more impactful than sex. It's actually quite a genius scheme. Humans instinctively run from, or at least avoid, what they fear. So, make them afraid to have sex. Tell them it's evil. Instill in them that sex equals sin—except, of course, in very specific circumstances. And yet, those same instincts hijacked by this doctrine are fundamental to our species. At the risk of oversimplifying, we know that humans are typically biologically wired to desire sex in order for the species to propagate. So, what happens when our *nature* overcomes the attempt to nurture this instinct out of us? We feel fundamentally flawed. Damned if I do; damned if I don't. Literally. And we grow up wondering why we have issues with intimacy! It would be comical if it wasn't so tragic.

In my church, children were introduced to the sacrament of Confession early. I think I might've been seven or eight the first time I had to disclose my *sins* to the priest. The premise of Confession is that you step into what seems like a small closet with some measure of anonymity and relieve yourself of guilt by confessing all the ways in which you have broken the "rules" of the religion. Then, after some conversation and questioning, the disembodied voice of the priest on the other side of a partition assigns you homework to repent for your sins. Say three *Hail Marys*, two *Our Fathers*, and you're good to go! I guess I should've found this comforting, but I didn't. Maybe I was foreseeing my future. I would learn decades later that divorce doesn't fit easily into this confessional construct. The whole setup is a little like a movie junket. The priest sits there in a position of authority, and congregants take turns sitting opposite him—one after another, as if deposited by a revolving door. Unlike the movie star, though, the priest asks the questions and, ideally, doles out forgiveness. Giving us a golden ticket that says GET OUT OF HELL FREE.

I was a sinner. Apparently, we all were. That's what my church told me. And I needed to confess my sins. Perhaps in compassion for our tender years, we were allowed to skip the dark booth. But that meant sitting in front of the priest in full view of the lineup of other children. A queue of sins waiting to be spoken. I'm not sure if the irony struck me, as I spent a full week beforehand creating a believable list. I needed three things that could meet the sacramental criteria without being considered hell-worthy. One: I yelled at my sister. Two: I stole a cookie without permission. True and true. Three: I picked some grapes out of the bowl without following my mother's rule of breaking them off in bunches so as not to leave unsightly stems. That last one was a fabrication, but the rule was real. Lying in confession...there must be a special part of Hell reserved for kids who do that.

Here's the truth I didn't tell: I was being abused.

An older boy was taking advantage of me. Touching me inappropriately. Making me touch him. A classic predator, he had access and opportunity in that time of free-range kids, and perhaps an instinct for the connection deficit I felt, the attention I craved. I never confessed this. I wonder what would've happened if I had. Instead, I packed my truth away. I denied it, erased it from my conscious memory. I let this shame become the secret foundation for a lifetime of self-flagellation. Of self-loathing. Hidden beneath my masks of social charm, wit, and achievement. I was ashamed it had happened, but beneath that was my deeper shame that I had not stopped it. I had allowed it. I buried this memory for a long time. But the shame was there waiting to surface—like a shark, silent and stealthy, menacing, waiting for an opportunity to attack.

I did not yet realize the adage *What doesn't kill you makes you stronger* is meaningless without healing. Because if you don't heal, you end up hurting others. And yourself. The excavation of my life eventually led me to this hard truth, but I only got there because of a willingness and courage to start digging again each time I had put down my shovel.

FINDING FORGIVENESS

I am
the tree of life
I will topple without strong roots
wither without connection
To grow
I must feed myself
forgiveness
Then love will flow
from the soil
of my life

Looping back to the distinction between self and story, these are just events that happened in my life; they are not who I am. I am not my wounds and neither are you, yours. I had to examine the story I've been told—and told myself—*about myself* in order to unravel it.

Will you dig down with me?

Start by asking yourself, what is there in your life—your story—that you would never tell anyone? If it's cloaked in secrecy, chances are it's enveloped in shame. The irony is that we protect these deep dark secrets thinking that will keep us safe, but the opposite is true. Recognizing their hold on us, and allowing ourselves to finally *process* these secrets, is how we open the door to freedom. As Brené Brown says, "Shame can't stand being spoken." Like any bully, shame relies on its victim staying a victim. Case in point: sharing this in a book would have long been inconceivable to me, but now that I am, it's shockingly liberating.

I'm not advocating speaking your shame to just anyone. Safety is key here. You must be in the presence of someone who will support you unconditionally, will keep your confidences, and is grounded enough to hold space for your pain without collapsing into their own. For many, that unique series of qualifications is only embodied in a therapist. That's also why I'm purposely not revealing all of my trauma in this book. I'm displaying what feels like a gargantuan amount of vulnerability in an effort to share the process that has freed me, the secret to my hard-earned ability to walk with my fear instead of running from it—in order to Show UP in a world that is often all about Showing Off.

Austrian neurologist and bestselling author Viktor Frankl says, "Between stimulus and response there is a space. In that space is our power to choose our response. In our response lies our growth and our freedom." Time is a continuum, and I believe that in sorting through the past to discover the obstacles to self-acceptance, I can re-respond to old stimuli. What happened in the past is in the past. It is no longer happening to me, so why should I allow it to continue to cause me pain? Yet this is what I've done for as long as I can remember. I carried a lifetime of uncomfortable responses (trauma) in the baggage that I dragged from place to place, chapter to chapter, relationship to relationship. And guess what? It gets in the fucking way. So, what if I take Frankl's brilliant concept and stretch it between a painful event of the past, and the present moment. See that gap, that space, as a gift—a renewed opportunity to respond. Make it a response that fuels rather than depletes me. Allows me to remember that I am the hero of my journey, not the victim.

I think it's fair to say that most people have suffered abuse of one kind or another—emotional, physical, sexual—and it all leaves scars. My personal process has been about unpacking trauma from my shame suitcase, exposing it to the sunlight, and laundering it; I begin by washing away the defective thought patterns attached to it—*It was my fault. I should've stopped it. I should've told someone.* Let me be clear though—this is self-work. I don't feel the need to actively engage anyone who has wronged me—and that's my choice to make—but I had to stop perpetrating my own punishment by wearing my shame. Forgiveness was, and is, an important part of that. Understanding and compassion had to come first, and that led me to the conclusion that, as the saying goes, "hurt people hurt people." I believe that older boy was a hurt person. In the vernacular of today, I don't know what had *happened* to him, but that's not a factor in my life. I trust he bore his own scars and acted out of his own pain. And for me, that conclusion opened the door to forgiveness.

Nelson Mandela taught the world a profound lesson in forgiveness by consciously letting go of anger toward his jailers after twenty-seven years of unjust imprisonment: "As I walked out the door towards the gate that would lead to my freedom, I knew if I didn't leave my bitterness and hatred behind, I'd still be in prison." Trying to live up to that kind of forgiveness is not the point here; the real lesson is in Mandela's assertion that prison is not just a place, but also a *mindset.* If we look at our own lives this way, our own shame, our own guilt, we recognize this important truth: we can be our own jailers. And in order to break out, we need to forgive ourselves.

Dr. Edith Eva Eger spent time in a different kind of captivity—as a prisoner in Auschwitz. Her book *The Choice* chronicles the horrors she experienced as a Jewish woman during the Holocaust, but it is centred around the mindset that enabled her to survive and heal, and ultimately help others through their own trauma by becoming a celebrated psychologist. "True freedom can only be achieved by choosing to let go, forgive, and move on," she says. That deeply held belief has fuelled a lifetime of helping others overcome trauma. Dr. Eger says that when it comes to suffering, there is no hierarchy. She asserts that judging ourselves in this way leads to minimizing our personal experience of trauma, and given what she's been through in her life, this is powerful permission:

> There's nothing that makes my pain worse or better than yours, no graph on which we can plot the relative importance of one sorrow versus another....If we discount our pain, or punish ourselves...then we're still choosing to be victims. We're not seeing our choices. We're judging ourselves.

This passage is meaningful to me because for so long, my privileged life was another weapon in the arsenal I used against myself. What the hell did I have to complain about? I was forever comparing my good fortune to the circumstances of others as yet another way to negate and suppress my own feelings. Despite living a relatively good life and having many opportunities that led to a fascinating career, I still fell victim to not-enoughness. Trapped in the dark pit of fear. That's the reason for this book. We are not here to belittle each other's traumas or compare them—that just gets us back to C&J. What we are here to do is to begin the life's work of digging ourselves out, and finding a way through those traumas. Whatever they may be.

And it's not a straightforward path. For this reason, I keep another passage from Dr. Eger's book posted on the wall of my office: "From this moment on, I understood that feelings, no matter how powerful, aren't fatal—and they are temporary. Suppressing the feelings only makes it harder to let them go. Expression is the opposite of depression." I read them often, and feel an enduring gratitude to their author.

A HOLE NEW PERSPECTIVE

I've used this dark hole metaphor as an opportunity to reveal some examples of old wounds. But since this journey takes us through the territory of my messy mind, it may not surprise you that it's a non-linear trip. Many of the personal revelations in this section are recent. They are the still-unfolding answers to the questions *What was holding me back?* and *Why did fear have such a hold on me?* As a former journalist, I consider the Five Ws—Who? What? When? Where? Why?—foundational in any type of inquiry. Now, a different question emerges that takes us on a fresh path with a whole new timeline: How? How did I manage to uncover and make sense of all this? It's not like my dig through the darkness was a straightforward affair. It's not like I uncovered these nuggets all at once—or even that I'm finished uncovering them. There were times when I got scared, when I lost my archaeological appetite, when I needed to regroup. There were also times when the busyness of everyday living got in the way. Perhaps the most reliable truth about the roller coaster of life is that there will be ups and downs. But once we're strapped in for the ride, we've got to be ready for it all. And sometimes, when we're stuck coasting downward, it can feel like a permanent trajectory.

The best explanation of depression I've ever seen is in the animated video of the book *I Had a Black Dog* by Australian author and artist Matthew Johnstone. It's based on Johnstone's own private experience with darkness in the midst of a highly successful career in advertising. The phrase "black dog" was made popular by another high-functioning man familiar with the drag of depression, Winston Churchill. It was actually an expression used by Victorian nannies (think Mary Poppins) to describe bad moods. In Johnstone's book and video, depression is presented as an actual dog that follows its owner everywhere, growing larger or smaller in relation to the severity of the owner's mental state. Most tellingly for me is when Johnstone, who narrates the video, says, "Because of the shame and stigma of the black dog, I was constantly worried I'd be found out. So I invested vast amounts of energy into covering him up."

I happen to have an actual black dog, a big Portuguese water dog named Hadley, but I've been fortunate to have only ever had a small black dog of depression. It never felt like mine. More like I was dog-sitting for a friend. I wouldn't have called it depression at the time—c&j made sure of that. I compared my situation to others, and judged myself unqualified to claim this title. And maybe I was afraid that if I admitted my secret state of unhappiness, I would have to show myself some compassion. Instead, I did the opposite. I beat myself up about feeling badly.

One day in my mid-forties, I took the enormous step of opening up the conversation with a doctor, and his response was quick and dismissive: "You're just going through a tough time" (which I was). "You'll be fine." I remember feeling frustrated that he didn't take my concerns seriously, but I also know my mask contributed to his reaction. I may not have seemed like a woman with depression, but I was struggling. One of my kids was navigating a serious health issue, and I felt like I was madly treading water, trying to keep my head above the surface.

I ended up in a therapist's office. It's important to note that I walked in wearing my cloak of confidence and would have initially appeared pretty composed. But it didn't take much to dissolve that impression. Here's how the session went:

> *Me:* "I don't know what's wrong with me. I'm a mess. I have a great life, and yet I'm on the verge of tears half the time and feeling anxious."
>
> *Therapist:* "Okay, why don't you tell me about yourself and what's been going on lately."

That may seem like a gentle and innocuous launchpad, but just knowing I was in a safe place with a professional who would keep my confidences opened the floodgates. I don't remember where I started, but I remember the tears. I cried my way through the next forty-five minutes as I detailed the obstacle course of challenges and losses I'd negotiated over the past decade. Had it been a movie, it would've been called *A Decade of Death & Divorce*. But it wasn't limited to those Ds. There was also the devastation of walking in and out of court with my dad when he was being tried for serious but decades-old allegations of sexual assault. Oh yeah...that.

I'm not going to get into details, but it was without a doubt a chapter of my life when I relied heavily on my mask. I was determined to demonstrate to the world that I was fine—partly because if I was fine, then it would stand to reason that he couldn't be guilty.

And to be clear, it did feel like the world was watching. It was a long way from the pageant runway, but that old fishbowl awareness of being judged hit a whole new level. Running the gauntlet of the flashing cameras and jockeying journalists of the national media each day, I had worn an expression of calm confidence; serious but not sad, interested but seemingly unaware of the circus erupting around me. *An excellent faker.* My father was acquitted of all the charges, but that wasn't the end of it. Suffice it to say it was a painful chapter, and that day in therapy, I reopened the wound. Let the blood flow.

I didn't know how much I'd been keeping bottled up inside me until I had this chance to let it out. After I had shared all the dire details of the past ten years, this therapist looked at me with a face full of compassion and asked, "So…do you still feel like you have no reason to feel overwhelmed?" It was a simple but powerful question. I felt a profound shift in my perspective, and actually started to laugh. It's like I had walked into her office dragging a black dog the size of a woolly mammoth and in the space of one hour, she had helped me *shrink* it.

I experienced a new sense of freedom that day. What I didn't realize at the time, however, was that I had reached the end of one chapter and the beginning of the next. I had felt for a long time like I was in a dark hole, but suddenly I saw the softest glimmer of light. And then I knew: it wasn't a hole at all, it was a tunnel.

TUNNEL

---

*"I saw Grief drinking a cup of sorrow and
called out, 'It tastes sweet, does it not?'
'You've caught me,' Grief answered, 'And
you've ruined my business. How can I sell sorrow when you know it's a blessing?'"*

—Rumi

Robert Frost was right. "The best way out is always through." Grief has convinced me of this. Losing ten close friends and family members in fifteen years seared this knowledge into my soul. It's indelible, like a tattoo—but the pain lasts a lot longer.

My grief is a well
When I lose someone, there is no containing it
Sadness spills over and fills the room
But in order to return to life
I must put a lid on it

Fastening it takes a gargantuan effort
like endeavouring to dam the sea

Eventually, though, the lid settles
—still blown open by the slightest breeze, but hinges in place

Time passes and the well rests
till one day...a comment, a memory, or a passing thought
lifts the lid

the depth of my pain
takes away my breath

I am unwell
till I am well again

One thing I'll say for suffering: it's a wake-up call. In the intro-duction to her extraordinary book *Broken Open*, Elizabeth Lesser makes the powerful observation that although life is character-ized by constant change, we humans seem programmed to resist it. She goes on to say, "And how ironic that the difficult times we fear might ruin us are the very ones that can break us open and help us blossom into who we were meant to be." We are often thrust into the darkness by circumstances beyond our control, but then we are confronted with a decision: remain stuck, or make a choice to move forward. For me, the only way to progress was through this existential tunnel. I had to accept life's invitation.

A lot of people resist this journey; they prefer the devil they know to the devil they don't. But for me, retreating wasn't an option. I knew that trying to climb my way up the slippery sides of that dark hole would only bring me more pain. I needed to follow the path toward light. I eventually discovered there were more choices to be made. As I was working my way through the tunnel,

I encountered clues that could lead to larger discoveries—but only if I *chose* to keep on digging in spite of the fear that, at times, seemed suffocating. As Dr. Eger puts it, "You can't change what happened, you can't change what you did or what was done to you. But you can choose how you live now...you can choose to be free."

An important part of making that choice to be free is learning to separate your self from your mind-chatter. Eckhart Tolle describes the moment when you realize there's a voice inside your head as "awakening out of your unconscious identification with the stream of thinking." In other words, realizing that *we are not our thoughts.* In my experience, when that awareness opens up within you, it's the beginning of a new sense of liberation, and the beginning of the end to the psychological imprisonment of victimhood. If your fears are suffocating you, it feels like you don't have options, but you do. And *choosing* converts reactions into responses. When I was rooted in fear, my reactions were fearful. Take jealousy for instance; when I didn't feel safe in a relationship, my reactions sprang from the threat I sensed. Whether that threat was real or not didn't matter, because my fear was. I had to learn how to step out of that long-held reflex and slide into the present moment to embrace choice. Eventually, meditation would give me the gift of presence, and help me finally grasp the distinction between my mind and my self. And that was crucial, because this next chapter of my journey required me to get out of my head and into my body.

When I find myself in this metaphorical tunnel now, when emotion rises, I know I've found a clue—a signpost of sorts: *More this way!* But the natural human inclination is to back away from anything painful—which in this case means swallowing the emotion and declining the invitation to understanding. Refusing to go deeper, trapped in our fear of what's there. These days, though, when I find even a fragment of a clue, I pick up my proverbial spade and start digging.

The process I'm describing reminds me of the time a friend's son fell and badly scraped his knee. It meant a trip to the ER, where a resident cleaned out the small pieces of gravel embedded in the boy's skin. Unfortunately, it wasn't a thorough job, and some pebbles were left behind. Two days later, my friend's son spiked a fever—it turned out he had swelling around the abrasion. Back in the hospital, a doctor said the infection was so bad that if they'd waited another day, the boy might've lost his leg. The way I see it, our emotional pain is like that gravel. Hard, jagged, and hidden, silently threatening until it can no longer be ignored. Trauma from childhood can be viewed in the same way. You just need to find the right kind of treatment that will help you learn to work through it—healing what you can, and learning to live with the scar tissue of what you can't.

GROUP DYNAMICS

"Once ready, I believe that sharing publicly from an anchored place within greatly accelerates our personal evolution. We free ourselves from painful guilt, life-sucking shame, and all the other low-vibrational emotions that come with feeling judged by ourselves. Once that is out of us, we become fearless and unstoppable. We do a great service as we free others from the limiting belief that they are alone in their suffering and we give them a silent permission to soften their own judgement about themselves and claim their own story, their truth..."
—Anne Bérubé, *Be Think Feel Do*

When I was younger and had my mask permanently affixed, I simply couldn't grasp the concept of group therapy. How could it work? Why would anyone want to talk about their fears and insecurities, let alone their trauma, in front of a group of strangers? Little did I know that this practice would hold a key to unlocking my own pain.

My first experience was in my mid-forties at the Kripalu Center for Yoga and Health in the Berkshire Hills of Massachusetts. There with a friend who was studying Yoga nidra, I had enrolled in a course on Freeing the Voice. I was attracted by the hope of literally freeing my voice, as I'd been plagued by recurrent laryngitis for years. But it turned out to be a much bigger opportunity.

We were a relatively small group—about fifteen participants, all women—and the course was led by a voice professional, who, as it quickly became obvious, was also spiritual. As we made our way around the circle sharing our stories, many of the participants revealed they were trauma survivors. By later that day, after a meditation exercise that had rooted us in the present moment (and in our bodies), we shared again, talking about what had come up for us through the deep breathing.

A woman started to speak vulnerably about the trauma of having her hearing damaged and living with torturous tinnitus (a constant ringing in her ears). She was a professional musician and music therapist, and as she spoke it was clear this was emotional territory for her. So far, I hadn't been sure how I felt about the whole *group* thing, but in that moment I sat transfixed by the energy in the room—as if our respectful attention, stillness, and silence had formed a safe container for her sharing. I listened intently to her words, but I was awestruck by her courage. Met with this supportive response from the group, her sadness and frustration suddenly came unharnessed, and she began to cry. That's when I felt a shift in my body, and my own emotion started to rise; it was like she had lifted the lid off my deep well. Her authentic presence had triggered mine. And her openness prompted a realization of my own.

In the group conversation that followed, I gently asked the woman if she felt that part of her trauma stemmed from her ability to hear (and make music) being connected to her definition of herself. She immediately registered a look of recognition, and what I saw on her face was exactly what I was feeling. I had just come to the conclusion that my own self-definition had a lot to do with my voice. So, who was I without it? That question provoked intense feelings of inadequacy, but for the first time I was in a place—both literally and figuratively—where I could take a long, hard look at this internal inferno.

Each day of the course, I felt myself cracking open a little more. I wrote this journal entry on day four.

Monday, May 21

If anyone ever told me that I would be sitting on the floor of this dorm room, soaking wet, methodically and reverently picking grass off my feet and sandals and placing it gently in a paper cup, I'm pretty sure I wouldn't have believed them! But that would have been B.L.—Before the Labyrinth.

Sandy and I took our lunch outside today and sat in those high-backed wooden chairs that we jokingly refer to as our "thrones." The main residence, which was once a monastery, is far from luxurious, but the property is magnificent. As we sat looking over the expanse of lush greenery, Sandy asked if

anyone had told me yet about the labyrinth. I said no, while
mentally scrambling to figure out if that was the same thing
as a maze. Sandy pointed down toward a lower point on the
property—a spot a little closer to the water we could see in
the distance. "Where that path is..." she said. Sure enough I
could see the start of a trail, which led into an area that was
obscured by an enormous tree. She explained briefly that
yes, a labyrinth is a little like a maze but with an important
distinction—which I really had to discover for myself. The
basic idea, though, was that you walk the path toward the
centre with an intention, and that many people find it gives
them great peace. I immediately thought about having heard
this morning that a new moon and a solar eclipse were going
to coincide this week and decided that even though I find it a
little woo-woo, it couldn't hurt to test the theory of a 48-hour
super-manifestation period around this momentous overlap in
the heavens! It might make my experience more powerful, or it
might not, but surely I had nothing to lose.

After lunch, Sandy went in to do some reading, and I
headed down to investigate. I felt like I was being drawn
toward the labyrinth like a magnet. It had been a sunny day
while we were eating but the skies had shifted and there was
one particularly ominous cloud moving into the picturesque
scene. Dark enough that it looked like it could open up and
release rain at any moment. But that didn't matter to me at all.
I felt this was the right thing at the right moment for me, and
as my feet landed on the little beaten path through the grass, a
sound rose lightly up to meet me. It was the sweet music of a
tin flute. I smiled as I realized it was coming from inside the
labyrinth. Sure enough, as I arrived at the gate that marks

the entrance, I discovered the instrument was being played by the woman in my class who'd had her hearing damaged. She was playing as she slowly walked the path. What a gift! My heart swelled with gratitude for the perfection of the moment. We smiled at one another, but since it was a contemplative endeavour, we resisted speaking.

I started my own walk, and soon discovered that the path doesn't make its way to the centre in a simple fashion (the circles don't just get progressively smaller). Instead, like my spiritual path, just when I'd think I was almost at the centre, it would take an unexpected turn and loop me back out to the periphery of the circle. As I walked, I focused on my footsteps and started repeating an intention to myself silently: "I release anxiety." Within seconds of saying it for the first time, I felt a drop of water on my face and thought, Now, wouldn't it be symbolic if it were to start raining right now? The Shakespearean atmosphere had already been set by the music that greeted my arrival, but now I was seeing a perfect example of what we had learned in high school was called pathetic fallacy—when nature reflects, through weather, internal turmoil or circumstances. This was a cleansing—within and without.

Again...perfection in the best sense of the word! As I made my way, the rain gradually grew more noticeable...until I reached the long-sought-after centre, and the skies opened up. In some ways, the best part was walking back out, retracing my steps and not rushing them at all—in spite of what had become pouring rain. As I finished and walked back out through the gate, I felt a new sense of calm. Then, as I headed up the hill with the awareness that I was soaked to the skin and would have to wring myself out before walking through

the residence, I started to laugh. I don't remember when I last
felt so relaxed, happy, and grateful.

Like my path to enlightenment (which I'm sure I'll be on till I die), that week was not a direct route, but it was a prelude to a kind of learning that would guide me through this tunnel, finally allowing me to make friends with my emotions—all of them! And because of that labyrinth experience specifically, *retreats* took on a whole new level of meaning for me. I was no longer lingering in the dark in stagnancy (*Stag-Nancy*), trying to find out what was wrong with me. All of a sudden, I was moving toward light. I will admit that, at times, it felt like it could've been the headlight of an oncoming train, but this newfound *motion* I'm talking about here was all about *e*-motion.

When you think about it, the word "emotion" itself tells us what to do with it. Move it. Cleaning out a horse's stall is often referred to as "mucking out" and that's an apt description of what needs to be done in the tunnel. And let me also say this: you can't just stir the shit around; you've gotta shovel it! And then, you've got to figure out how to process that shit.

EMBODIED EMOTION

Feelings are for feeling. These simple words are on the wall of the writing room of bestselling author Glennon Doyle, but when you consider how we humans resist fully feeling, the message isn't simple at all—not until you allow yourself to learn that it really is the easiest path. Like unblocking a dam in a river, allowing the flow of emotion turns out to be the most natural thing in the world.

But man, oh man, dismantling that damn dam requires work!

The concept of Embodied Emotion was a game changer for me. Ultimately, it's a straightforward process, but before you understand it, it can seem like the hardest thing in the world. That's where a facilitator comes in, and Anne Bérubé was my conductor through this crucial part of my journey. Anne and I first met through our husbands. For five years, I'd worked on an annual fundraiser with Anne's partner, Paul, and he and I had become fast friends, but it was three years in before I met Anne. My husband met her first; he came home from an event raving about how I needed to meet Paul's wife. His instinct was dead-on, and in the years since, Anne has become one of my closest connections, personally and professionally. She's a soul sister who has taught me so much, but she started as my student. She came to me for guidance, as she was transitioning from being a producer to a speaker.

At the time, I was going through my own transition. After leaving television, I had created a business working as a flexible freelancer, MCing, speaking, and acting, and I had landed a regular gig writing a profile column for a local paper, which I loved (until the paper went under!). I also occasionally offered media training. To me, helping people hone their public message sometimes felt contrived, but it led me to discover how much I loved helping clients feel more comfortable *delivering* their ideas. And that led me to presentation training. Anne was my first legit client on this new path.

Let me back up for a moment and share a quick story that speaks volumes about Anne. Although she was firmly set on establishing a career in academia in her early twenties, a car accident radically changed her trajectory. She was badly injured, and in the crucial moments after impact, she saw a vision of her life that was entirely different than the conventional one she was living. This unexpected awakening led to a whole new path, professionally and personally. As I see it, it was a sharp pivot from Showing Off to Showing UP.

Seven years later, Anne was married to the love of her life (Paul) and was learning to allow purpose to drive her career. At the time, Paul's parents owned a seaside resort in Nova Scotia, and Anne began hosting small gatherings there where people could engage in soulful exploration. She set her sights on amplifying the voices of spiritual leaders, and all at once, her mission and ambition combined to create magic. After reaching out to several internationally known speakers, she made a cold call to Deepak Chopra's agent, and somehow convinced him she could produce an event in Halifax for Chopra's minimum audience—over one thousand people. Her biggest audience to date had been about fifty, but she succeeded with flying colours. That first Deepak Chopra event catapulted Anne and Paul into success in this new venture, and just like that, they became event producers. They continued to work with Chopra on numerous occasions, but their reputation would also lead to a close working relationship with another of the world's most successful authors, Dr. Wayne Dyer.

Enter Nancy, stage left. Anne came to me looking for help with her stage presence and speaking style as she was preparing to take on a more significant role on Wayne's upcoming tour in eastern Canada. It would be her first time publicly stepping into the spotlight, and she definitely needed some polishing. Our interaction proved to be a huge success for both of us. She was a great student, and seeing dramatic improvement as I worked with her, I realized that I was a great teacher, too. I was intuitive, a good communicator, and I was having fun! This was the kind of work I'd been longing for. Anne is also a teacher—a transformative one. My new connection to her eventually led to something else for which I'd been starving: a better relationship with myself. But to get there, I had some work to do.

Anne's approach to emotion is summed up in her first book, *Be Feel Think Do*. At that time, it was still in manuscript form and she was looking for a publisher, but she'd been sharing her process with clients for years. Here's the gist of it: we all spend so much time *doing* in our busy world, and that renders our *thinking* frenetic, so we rarely allow ourselves to *feel*, and almost never create opportunities to just *be*. Anne's theory involves flipping that order and making *be* the priority. All of a sudden, that facilitates a willingness to *feel*, which changes the way we *think*, and positively impacts our *doing*—and ultimately, this changes the way we show up in the world.

As an embodied emotion facilitator, Anne helps people learn how to *feel*; or more accurately, how to embrace and get comfortable feeling the full range of human emotion. And her secret weapon is something so simple, so elemental, that most people resist the possibility that it can be so powerful.

BREATH & E-MOTION

As Joseph Pilates so eloquently says, "Breathing is the first act of life and the last." And yet most of us, he adds, "have never mastered the art of correct breathing." That's significant on a physical and psychological level, and here's my personal metaphor for explaining why: I think of my body as a highway—and my emotions within as a bus. Only when I let go, and practice fully inhaling and fully exhaling, in a state of presence, can I let my breath move the bus, move me. When my bus is in motion, it allows me to exhale the negative emotion I've got trapped inside me—the exhaust. But the moment I put the air brakes on, the bus stops in its tracks. Then it's just a huge lump in my stomach, my heart, or my throat.

There's a classic old *Saturday Night Live* skit called "Coffee Talk," in which Canadian comedian Mike Myers plays a stereotypical Jewish mother who hosts a talk show. In the midst of each "show," she would inevitably become emotional about some topic, and that's when the famous line was uttered—in a strong New York accent—"I'm getting a little verklempt! Talk amongst yourselves." It was one of those gems of comedic genius that made its way into everyday conversations. I had no idea first time I heard it what the word "verklempt" meant, but I certainly knew the feeling. In fact, I was an expert at it. I had been practicing swallowing my feelings since I was a kid. Of course, that made me just like almost everybody else. And I think that's part of the reason the skit resonated. It tapped into a universal human condition. "Verklempt" is a Yiddish word that means *overwhelmed by emotion, choked up, or clenched.* That last one hits home for me. I spent a lifetime clenching against rising emotion. It was a well-established habit that was reinforced by my perfectionism, my mask, and my fear.

Hindsight really is 20/20, and I can see clearly now what was going wrong. I am an empath—I was built to be a *path* for emotion! I was born to be a bus driver, and instead I was the owner of a broken-down bus. I wasn't going anywhere. What I learned so powerfully from Anne, is that breath is essential to the animation of this e-motion. *"Wait a second,"* you might say, *"we are all breathing all the time. We have to breathe to stay alive!"* That's true, but there's a huge difference between the amount of oxygen you require to live, and the amount your body actually craves. It's like water. You can *live* on a few sips a day, but that's far from what your body needs for optimum health—physically or emotionally. Returning to our full-bodied breath, the way we breathed when we were babies, fuels the bus and gets emotion moving.

For many of us, our natural reaction when we start to *feel* is to freeze. Catch that sadness, anger, or whatever else is rising, and clench it. Slam on the brakes. In one of my early sessions with Anne, she asked me, "When was the last time you cried until you were done?" Those words landed right in my heart. And my heart answered: "What? You mean that's an option?!" Let me ask you the same: When was the last time you cried...*until you were done?* Don't get me wrong, this work is not all about crying, but when you decide to release that lifetime of emotion you've stuffed inside, it can get messy. I speak from first-hand experience. It got messy for me in Turks and Caicos.

The retreat was called the Celestial Sessions, and Anne was hosting it at a rustic North Caicos resort. It was more like a motel really, but it was the perfect setting for this adventure. Our group of twelve welcomed the sunrise waist-deep in the turquoise ocean, and marvelled at the Milky Way at night. During the day, though, we had work to do. Our sessions were held in an open-air hut with a roof of palm leaves on the edge of the beach, and we were only about twenty feet from the shoreline. I think you've got the picture: it was paradise. Not the manicured version you might see on a brochure, but the real deal.

I had set an intention on this trip to get *real*—with others and with myself. And that's what happened. Inspired by what I had witnessed at Kripalu, and feeling safe and supported, I shared with the group more of my story than I'd ever been able to share with anyone before. I wasn't alone in that; there was some radical honesty going on—it was like we were stripping away our personas and unmasking in front of each other. Later that day, I discovered the sheer truth in what Brené Brown means when she says, "shame cannot survive being spoken."

We were in the middle of a guided meditation when I started to feel a wave of emotion—the same wave I had been resisting my whole life. This time, though, I was ready to ride it. I started to cry, feeling surprisingly unselfconscious. The rest of the group kept breathing while Anne honed in on me as she continued speaking, fixing my eyes with her steady and loving gaze. She knew what was about to happen: a guided meltdown! I started to sob, and although my natural inclination was to close my eyes and stop, Anne reminded me to keep my eyes open. I knew, from having watched her work with others, that this was designed to help me stay in the moment and out of my "story." Unlike talk therapy, embodied emotion is not working through what caused the feelings, but about *allowing* the movement of energy and information through my body.

So, there I was, tears streaming down my face, desperately trying to surf on what was becoming a tidal wave. It felt like too much. All of a sudden, things got weird. My hands started seizing up, curling in awkwardly. Then my arms followed suit; I couldn't straighten them out. I started to panic. And that's when I saw a hint of a smile appear on Anne's face, and it flipped a switch in me. I was standing there partially paralyzed by this bizarre occurrence, but I was somehow still obediently breathing, and all of a sudden I felt utter trust in her and in the process.

I cried until I was done.

Have you ever felt the relief of throwing up after you've been nauseous all day? That's the best way I can describe this experience—like I vomited out every bit of fear, anxiety, and shame I'd been harbouring. I began to laugh through my tears. And then I was overcome with a different kind of wave, one of pure joy. I had to move. Without explanation or apology, I bolted from the circle, hopped over the railing and into the sand, and ran, fully dressed and at full speed, straight into the water.

So, why was Anne smiling while I was a blubbering snotty mess? Because she knew I had to "feel it to heal it," and that the freedom on the other side of that discomfort would be well worth it. That I had to breathe through the pain. She was so right, and it's physically impossible for me now to keep a smile off *my* face when I think about how liberated I felt floating in the ocean at that pivotal moment. Like I had been madly treading water all my life and was suddenly buoyant.

When I quizzed Anne afterwards about what the heck had been going on with my arms, she had a matter-of-fact explanation: I had experienced a release of old beliefs surrounding my identity; that this was delivered through a heart-chakra opening, and that my arms were affected because they're part of that chakra. (Lift yours so that they're shoulder-level, and that'll make more sense.)

It's only when you stop banging your head against the wall that you understand what it's like not to feel the pain it causes. How much better life is without that destructive pattern. This is how I felt about stepping out of my fear and my armour. It was the moment I realized how much my life had been about control. This was the start of a new paradigm, the foundation of which is this discovery: *Fear controls. Love allows.* Here's the visual that goes with that motto: let's go back to that image of life as a roller coaster. If you're stiff with fear, you're way more likely to get whip-lash. If you relax and *allow*, you can enjoy the ride.

The bizarre thing about embodiment is that it's a foreign con-cept to many in a world replete with so much anxiety. We absorb negative energy, we live it, we suffer because of it, but we don't process our feelings about it.

my cheeks are stained with tears today
emotion rolls through me in waves
but I'm not afraid of the sorrow I feel
it's been building for too many days

some sadness is mine and the rest for the world
all the pain and the suffering I see
allowing this feeling won't solve all the woes
but it does help me to be free

When I was in my mid-twenties, a boyfriend of mine broke up with me and moved away. I was pretty smitten with him, and with everything our relationship represented. Hindsight has shown me that acceptance and belonging were wrapped up in that bond, and I realize now the impact of that sense of desertion I felt. It triggered my abandonment issues and brought me face to face with my own not-enoughess. But at the time, it just felt like my world was falling apart. I actually called in sick to work for a week! I lied to my boss, telling him a friend had died. Because that's how it felt. I couldn't stop crying, and I was way too embarrassed to tell the truth—not only had I been "dumped," but I was an uncon-trollable emotional mess. To make things worse, said boyfriend revealed that he was leaving to be with his old girlfriend. While this made everything seem much worse at the time, I can now sit in gratitude for the extra measure of pain it provoked. Because it was a flashpoint in my life.

What do most of us do when we experience an emotional body blow like this? We may cry our eyes out, even yell and scream into the abyss, as we absorb the full force of the pain. But then, we shut that process down as soon as we are able. In the same way we bury any tangible mementos of our defunct romance, we pack away the tears, memories, and torment. But here's the thing I've learned: holding onto that shit isn't healthy.

I didn't learn the lessons this experience had to teach me for a long time. Because as soon as I could, I stuffed the heartache in boxes in my psyche and duct-taped them shut. I thought that was how a strong person "deals with it." Sitting here writing these words thirty years later, I chuckle at the perfection of this analogy. The pain I packed away remained with me for decades—like those boxes you move from house to house and never get around to opening. That lost love got in the way of me forming healthy bonds for *years*—because of how I allowed it to erode my own sense of self; how I let it confirm my fear that I was not worthy of love. There was a time I might have told you I hated that young man, but I've come back around to loving him for the role he played in my undoing. Negative emotions, like boxes of clutter, can only be hidden or buried for so long. Eventually they have to be released.

I got a personal masterclass in processing pain from a dear friend who suffered a monumental betrayal at the hands of her husband of thirty years. She discovered he'd been having an affair for two-thirds of their marriage, a marriage she considered success-ful—not without bumps in the road, but based on a real, honest, and deep connection. The revelation of her partner's infidelity left her in ruins, like a house with the foundation ripped out from beneath it.

Her process of rebuilding taught me a valuable lesson in emotional transport because of her extraordinary willingness to sit with her own sorrow. Having walked a path of self-exploration throughout much of her life, she ventured bravely into the abyss. Like any grief, she realized she had to go through that dark tunnel to get to the other side, even though I imagine there were days she doubted she'd ever make it. *She cried until she was done.*

Here's where I learned my greatest lesson, and realized the truth of Ram Dass's beautiful saying, "We're all just walking each other home." While my friend demonstrated for me the true beauty and healing power of embodied emotion, I was also able to give her a gift—from the universe. After having spent a few days with her while on business in her city, I boarded a plane for home. The moment we lifted off, a poem landed. I knew without a doubt that it was for her.

A shocking gift
a present
of pain
Betrayal
becomes a stubborn stain

The grief is large
the tunnel dark
Sorrow
suffocates
her broken heart

Time must pass
and anger rise
like a sharpened blade
to cut old ties

The jaguar prowls
in her soul
healing
the wound
The spirit's still whole

A path appears
as if from above
The Universe whispers
Follow the love

ALLOWING ANGER

"Heav'n has no rage, like love to hatred turn'd,
Nor hell a fury, like a woman scorn'd."
—Zara in Act III, Scene II, *The Mourning Bride*

I have learned that often before we can be comfortable in our own skin, we've got to let ourselves embrace our anger. I used the words "internal inferno" earlier to describe my own emotional turmoil, and that's really how I think of my anger. I've learned that freedom is found not in avoiding the intensity, but allowing it.

Anger is an apt example of the distinction between healthy and unhealthy emotional expression. For many years I disowned my anger. I didn't want to accept that it belonged to me. So, you know how it showed up? Uncontrollably. When I "lost control." Rumi's line "The wound is where the light enters" has always resonated for me, but I have definitely known the flip side of that coin as well. If you don't tend to it, the wound is how the darkness (or anger) *gets out*.

Anger is a valid emotion, but it is only helpful to me if I exercise it when I'm in a state of presence. And the opposite of presence is absence. When I am absent, my anger is destructive; it is disembodied like a hurricane, whipping around debris. Someone in such a state could be labelled "out of their mind," but I think of it as being trapped *in* my mind and detached from my heart. And my emotion is released in explosive bursts that feel out of my control.

Embodied anger, on the other hand, is righteous and rightful. Acknowledging and respecting it goes a long way to channelling it properly. Breathing through it while grounded. Using it as fuel. I think of myself as a volcano. If I make a practice of regularly letting off steam, I can live reasonably calmly as a solid mountain with fire inside me. It animates me. But if, as the steam builds, I contain it in an attempt to control everything, eventually it's going to blow! It's easy to tell the difference between embodied and disembodied fire. The latter causes collateral damage for innocent bystanders. Embodied fire is constructive. It's a true expression of emotion, often in response to injustice, unfairness, or cruelty.

As I write this, I think of my anger at the recent discovery of the thousands of children in unmarked graves at the sites of former Indian Residential Schools in Canada. Children who were taken forcibly from their parents and families and stripped of their Indigenous cultures and languages. My heart goes out to the survivors of those "schools." How scared they must have been, just children, separated from their families, elders, and communities.

And the unimaginable scars they must carry from the legacy of psychological, physical, and sexual abuse. We all walk through this world with wounds, and there's a horrifying scale from scratches to open lacerations, but no matter where you land on the spectrum of suffering, never forget that your trauma is real to you. And it may well have impact in your life whether you're aware of it or not.

If I can feel insecurity, fear, and anger as the result of unprocessed issues from my white privileged past, I can't even imagine the torment of those who have been harshly excluded from society, fed a constant diet of "you are less than us," and denied a sense of connection and belonging. But Showing UP fully, I need to say that my anger at what happened in Canada's residential schools has an added dimension of guilt. A feeling of complicity that I didn't sit up and take notice until now. I knew the prejudice and racism existed, but it didn't directly impact my life. That is a hard thing to say. To write. To admit. But it's true. I had a similar reaction when George Floyd was murdered in 2020.

Atrocities like these deserve our anger and sadness. This kind of anger, when collective, can be constructive—it can lead to rallies, new policies, holding perpetrators to account, and fighting for justice for those wronged. But when you're already feeling anger on a personal level, the feelings created by these watershed social moments can sometimes compound what we're already feeling, leading to a sense of deep helplessness and non-constructive anger.

I've heard depression described as "anger turned inward" and that's always felt accurate for me. Like a poison boiling away inside me with no outlet. Not a poison I was fed, but the fermented result of bottling up my natural fire energy. As children, we're often not allowed to experience the full extent of our emotions. Adults routinely interrupt the expression of our fire. When our natural flame erupts—whether in anger, excitement, or even joy—they all too often seek to dampen or extinguish it. To give them the benefit of the doubt (particularly as I am a parent and I have done this), I'd suggest that in most cases, parents may just be trying to control their children's fire so they don't get burned by society. But in attempting to make their kids conform, saying things like "Don't cry"; "You're bad"; "You're too much" is the equivalent of dumping flame retardant on them. These kinds of statements eventually become the patter of our inner critic. You could say, the old model of parenting was very much about firefighting.

I certainly wasn't allowed to embody those fiery emotions, so they got shut down. It wasn't safe to be sad, angry, or depressed— because of our parents' generation's approach to emotional outbursts. Not proper. Unacceptable. Bad behaviour. Problem child. As Kathy Bates's character says to her feisty elderly friend in the movie *Fried Green Tomatoes*, "I never get mad, Miss Threadgoode, never. The way I was raised, it was bad manners!" Let me be clear here: I am not blaming my parents or yours. They were parented this way, their parents were parented this way, and so on and so on. I don't hold them responsible, but I'm keen to break this pattern.

I remember one Christmas as a kid spent in a rented house on a family ski trip. I was upset about something and opted out of going downstairs to supper. This was not a popular choice. I know it seems like a hilariously minor rebellion but, people pleaser that I was, I wasn't used to being defiant. I have an enduring memory of my father, who rarely got angry, storming up to my room and ordering me to join the family downstairs to "eat that supper your mother has made!" I stood up to him, saying I wasn't feeling well

and preferred to stay in bed. But then I got yelled at, and immediately caved. Yelling back wasn't an option. Neither was talking
back. I was mad, but I did what a good girl would do: I slunk down
to join the family. I'm sure I sulked my way through the meal, but
I swallowed my anger because I had no choice—and that's about
all I ate that night.

Chances are, you don't have to dig deep to come up with a more
traumatic childhood memory of your emotions being steamrolled.
But here's why this story is significant to me. As a young empath, I
was attempting to honour my own instincts and boundaries, and
the adult response was typical of that generation: *"You do what I
say, now."* No room for offspring sovereignty in that parenting philosophy. The gist of it is simple: *We adults decide what you do, where
you go, and we will tell you how to feel.* So-called "negative" feelings
are neither encouraged nor even tolerated in this model, except in
moments of extreme pain, dismemberment, or bloodletting. Oh,
and if you're a boy, forget about it! (That's a whole other book!).
Being raised with the understanding that we're not entitled to
our emotions leads us into a natural pattern of negating them. It's
only now, looking back through this magic tunnel of mine, that
I realize not only did I negate any feelings of sadness and anger I
encountered, I allowed those feelings to make me feel more shame.
And sure enough, in my early years of parenting, I fell into the trap
of perpetuating the same pattern with my own kids.

I remember taking my first son to Florida to visit my parents
when he was about eighteen months old. He was a pretty easygoing
baby, and he travelled well, but being in a different environment had
always wreaked havoc on his—and therefore my—sleep. This was
probably his first time spending an extended period of time away
from home, and he seemed to be adjusting well. Until the third day,

when we went to visit friends of my parents. Everything was fine at first; he was his charming self, playing happily, and I was quite content to accept the accolades for my well-behaved child. Then suddenly his mood turned on a dime—he went from perfect child to perfectly horrid. His meltdown quickly triggered the resurrection of my old nemesis: WWTNT (What will the neighbours think)?! All of a sudden, I went from proud Mama Bear to Skunk Mama—the one ultimately responsible for this child's stinky behaviour.

Over my twenty-five years of parenting, I have definitely suppressed my children's fire, each to a different degree, and that had everything to do with my own fear of inadequacy. As babies, from our first cry in the delivery room, we let our voices be heard and our emotions be known. Parenthood in a world of Comparison and Judgement (C&J) means we're programmed to believe that quiet babies are good babies and, therefore, crying babies are bad babies. I've watched countless mothers shrink in shame publicly because their child was crying inconsolably. I recognize that reaction because I remember the feeling. As I see it, here's the simple structure of this cascade:

1. My baby is bad
2. I'm a bad mother
3. I'm not enough
4. I'm ashamed that the world knows my secret

I've been there. But let's get real: that baby is simply expressing discomfort. And here's where the stick gets thrust into the spokes. As humans, we are meant to allow emotion to move through our bodies. We are pros at this when we're infants, because it is *natural* to us. We never have to learn this behaviour. But the adults of the world, who have all forgotten how to live this way, continue the cycle by teaching their children—from a very early age—to repress their emotions. Even as we're just blossoming into ourselves as toddlers, the world endeavours to rein us in.

Expression is allowed
for only so long
till Repression
shadows our light
but there in the dark
without movement or flow
our emotions forget
where to go

Like a freezer for feelings
depression ensues
as numbness
takes over our being
The only solution
in this cruel evolution
is to turn round and find what is freeing

Go back where we started
before the distress
and re-open ourselves
to
express

It's true what they say: our children are our greatest teachers. But sometimes it takes decades to understand the learning they've offered up. My second son navigated his early childhood with his emotional gauge on full throttle. When he was having fun, he'd declare gleefully that he was *so happy*—much to the bemused delight of adults around him. When sad, he was equally forthcoming—though he'd often admit he didn't know why. He was a master of expression.

For me, opening up took a lot of courage because it meant lowering my mask. Dismantling my castle. And GUS really didn't like that idea. Living in the public eye had given me good reason to be protective. Apart from dreading the constant judgement of my audience, I was also the frequent target of a local would-be tabloid that regularly presented fiction as fact. But there was a much more serious threat that helped to fuel my fear—something I never expected. Stalkers.

Being a big frog in a small pond too often attracted the wrong kind of attention. During my time on TV, I experienced this a number of times. It got to the point where the person who ran the station's mailroom was instructed to open all letters and packages addressed to me before handing them over. That way, I wouldn't be weighed down by worry about threats to my safety, and I wouldn't be aware of how many of my fans veered toward *fanatic*.

My most traumatic experience with stalking ended in court after the police discovered weapons in the perpetrator's house. When asked why he had them, the man calmly explained that he needed to protect himself. "From who?" asked the cops. "From the Regans and ATV," was his reply. It turns out he had paranoid schizophrenia, and watching me every night on television had enabled a delusion that he and I were in a relationship. He was utterly convinced that my employer and family had kidnapped and brainwashed me so that I couldn't remember I loved him. He was found guilty, but "not criminally responsible" because of his mental illness.

This is just one example of many. So, it's not surprising that my relationship with fear took on a whole new dimension in that stage of my life. At the time, though, I hid how much this all scared me, and that meant that my mask became even more important— my armour needed to be reinforced. I fortified my castle instead of opening up. Vulnerability was a foreign country to me and I never even wanted to visit it, let alone live there. Learning to embrace it is what ultimately helped me move through my tunnel toward self-acceptance.

TRUE CONNECTION

I want to take you back to the work of Brené Brown now because what I've learned from her about the power of connection has changed my life. Her research has shown that we can only achieve authentic connection when we allow ourselves to be authentic with others. But it was a book she wrote before fame found her that first impacted me. *The Gifts of Imperfection* was another gift from the universe that landed in my life just when I was ready for it. It delivered the powerful message that perfectionism is a *prison*:

> Owning our story can be hard but not nearly as difficult as spending our lives running from it. Embracing our vulnerabilities is risky but not nearly as dangerous as giving up on love and belonging and joy—the experiences that make us the most vulnerable.

What this means to me is that only when we are brave enough to explore the darkness will we discover the infinite power of our light. The harsh reality this quote highlights is that my instinct to protect myself also disconnected me from the richness of human connection.

Growing up, I never felt comfortable in a group of girls. There was too much jockeying for power, too much C&J. Though the other girls probably never would have guessed it, I was always self-conscious about whether I fit in—it was like playing defence all the time. *Keep your centre of gravity low and be prepared to shift direction quickly.* I chose to actually play defence—and offence— on the basketball court instead, and I particularly loved playing with the boys because there was so much less drama.

As I aged, my relationships suffered from my inclination to maintain a safe distance. I had good friends, but none with whom I could share my deepest feelings. Connection and belonging, as Brené puts it, are "fundamental human needs," but when you feel less-than, there's a tendency towards isolation. Even in a crowd, you can feel alone. Vivek Murthy, the US Surgeon General, has a unique perspective on this. Fortunately for us, he shared them in his book, *Together: The Healing Power of Human Connection in a Sometimes Lonely World,* and he summed it up on Brené's podcast, *Unlocking Us*:

> When I looked back at all the issues I was dealing with as Surgeon General—whether it was addiction, or whether it was violence, or whether it was obesity or whether it was depression and anxiety, I realized that the root of so many of these was loneliness and part of the solution for so much of it was actually human connection.

Across the pond in 2018, the UK revealed similar findings that painted a bleak picture: an epidemic of connection-deficit. Then-prime minister Theresa May decided to address this creatively, at a governmental level, creating the first Ministry of Loneliness. It was formed in part as a reaction to the tumult and stress of Brexit, but was also based on research that showed nine million Britons—14 percent of the population—suffer from loneliness, data that was compiled in a report called the *Jo Cox Commission on Loneliness.* It cast a light on the darkness so many were living in—particularly the elderly, those with disabilities, young people, parents, carers and migrants.

There were lots of jokes made about this new ministry on both sides of the Atlantic. Stephen Colbert described it as "so British," saying, "They've defined the most ineffable human problem and come up with the most cold, bureaucratic solution." But if you look beyond the humour, there's no arguing that loneliness is a serious social challenge and a serious health risk. According to the Jo Cox report, "weak social connection is as harmful to health as smoking 15 cigarettes a day" and "loneliness costs UK employers £2.5 billion a year." The problem needs addressing, and it's hardly unique to British society. As Mother Teresa, who dedicated her life to working with the poor, once said, "Loneliness and the feeling of being unwanted is the most terribly poverty."

Here's my takeaway. The medicine we so desperately need is often right in front of us, but without authenticity and vulnerability we can't access it. It's like having a prescription for a wonder drug that might save your life but not being able to figure out the child-proof cap. I have learned first-hand that when we share only our masks with others, they share theirs with us. We don't see past the surface. Showing Off blocks our perceived flaws and weaknesses from being seen; it protects our vulnerabilities, but it also hides our true selves. And this intensifies isolation. When I reveal my softer side, the part of me I'm reluctant to show to the world for fear of being judged, I open myself up to the softer side of others.

I do feel like there's an important distinction to be made here, because getting real with people around you is not the same as complaining. I've known people who base the openness of their friendships on being transparent about what drives them crazy about others, themselves, the world. Complaints and c&j are not the stuff of the soul. They are launched from an ego level of mind. So, in a way, they create *fear friends* instead of dear friends.

Brené Brown has a beautiful motto that she shares on each episode of her podcast, and it hits me in the solar plexus every time: "Strong back, soft front, wild heart." This says it all. You can navigate life as a strong human and even hold power, while also being compassionate and open, and embodying an adventurous approach to life that is connected to your wild child within.

For me, it was often easier to be vulnerable with people I'd just met. I have vivid memories as an adult of trying to share my insecurity with those close to me and being shut down. Being told I was being ridiculous—that I had never lacked confidence, that I was the paragon of self-esteem. I can't blame them for this distorted belief because I'd been crafting my mask since childhood. Furthermore, they were right—to an extent. That's where paradox comes into the picture.

PARADOX

Elizabeth Gilbert laid some vital tracks in my tunnel during the conversation we recorded for my podcast *The Soul Booth.* In fact,

I almost think of her as a switcher—because something she said changed my direction, moving me onto the track of accepting both myself and those around me. She introduced the concept of *paradox* into my life in a fresh and formidable way.

But first I had to experience a familiar tailspin. I was standing in the middle of a luxurious flat on New York's Upper East Side, but psychologically I was on my way to a much less desirable location: the Land of Fear and Doubt. *What if I don't do a good job? What if she doesn't like me? Maybe I'm not ready for this.* "Whoa, Nancy! Rein it in, girl!" I interrupted my slide by saying this out loud, drowning out any echoes of the bullies that used to terrorize me, and I actually made myself laugh. If you've made it this far, you know those old negative voices were my own. I was in the midst of catching myself in an old pattern as I waited for one of my favourite authors to arrive. Here's the thing: I do still get caught in that old vortex, but through the practice of presence, I've learned to change the channel. And I got busy doing just that.

I sat myself down, took off my shoes, and focused on my breath. I recognized those old self-limiting beliefs and greeted them with compassion. Slowly but surely, I pulled out of that negative spiral and rooted myself in the legitimate enthusiasm I felt. Then I used another tool I've acquired over the years. I invited gratitude into the room—because, as I've discovered, it is impossible to be stressed and grateful at the same time. By the time Liz Gilbert arrived for our recording, the nervous butterflies were flying in formation; I was ready. It helped immensely that Anne had come along to operate my cameras, and she also acted as "greeter" and met this world-famous author on the sidewalk outside—also in her bare feet. As soon as Liz walked in, she kicked off her own shoes, and we settled into the plush velvet couch for an intimate conversation.

Just before we started, I joked that I would have to relegate my inner fangirl to the corner of the couch. Her response surprised me: "You bring every part of you to this conversation, and I'll bring every part of me." And that's just what we did. What followed was an organic exchange of ideas, and a deep dive into the topic of embracing a fearless and creative life.

If you look in the dictionary under "creativity," Elizabeth Gilbert's photo might be there. From the time she was a child, writing has been her passion and purpose. Of course, she's best known for her bestselling 2006 memoir, *Eat, Pray, Love.* Here's the synopsis in case you missed it: Liz's marriage breakdown triggers an emotional crisis and spawns a journey that begins as phys- ical (food) in Italy but morphs into a spiritual journey in India. Eventually, she lands in Bali, where she finds a new relationship. But it's a love story with a difference, because it's really about Liz learning to love herself. That's what made some critics, like the *New York Post*, label the book "narcissistic new-age reading" but it's also why it resonated with millions of women around the world, including me. Her unique brand of radical authenticity, charm, and laugh-out-loud humour earned the book 199 weeks on the *New York Times* bestseller list, and in 2010 it became a hit film star- ring Julia Roberts.

It's no surprise that love surfaced early in our conversa- tion. "All I want to do," Liz said, "is give people permission slips—for everything. Not just permission to create, or to change their lives, or to do dramatic, exciting, positive things... but also permission to be broken and insecure, and lost and scared and needy, and all of that gets to have space too. The room of love lets everything in." Since the runaway success of *Eat, Pray, Love*, Liz has had lots of experience with love—and being broken. Her romantic life has been complicated, but she's been consistent in staying true to herself, and she has willingly weathered the triumphs and sorrows publicly. Her commitment to vulnerability fits in perfectly with the view of fear she espouses in her 2015 book about the art of creation, *Big Magic*.

This book rocked my world, with its assertion that creativity, like a life fully lived, is not neat and tidy, and that curiosity should be the engine that drives us. Reading it was a welcome reminder that fear too often controlled my every move, and whether it was fear of failure, judgement, or not being enough, it not only prevented me from creating art, it also kept me from connection. "Fear is always triggered by creativity," she explains in the book, "because creativity asks you to enter into realms of uncertain outcome, and fear hates uncertain outcome. This is nothing to be ashamed of. It is, however, something to be dealt with."

When I mentioned to two women at the gym that I was going to New York City to interview Liz Gilbert, they both reacted strongly. One of them cited *Eat, Pray, Love* as a book that changed her perspective on life and opened her up to more joy; the other remembered abandoning it halfway through, utterly disgusted by the "self-absorbed" tale. Their individual reactions reminded me of how public opinion used to haunt me. That's why it's inspiring to see how Liz steps out into the world. She steadfastly refuses to live her life according to the expectations or critique of others.

Our conversation took a natural turn into the subject of paradox—which, as I came to understand that day, can be a magic key to unlocking self-compassion. Liz launched into it with this: "Somebody said to me once, when it comes to inspiration and creativity, 'Do you believe inspiration comes from the Divine and channels through you, or do you believe in hard work?'" She paused and then continued:

> I said...yes! That's kind of my position on most things. The eternal paradox: do you believe in free will or destiny? Yes. Do you believe true love should be clear and obvious and automatic, or do you believe that relationships are hard work? Yes! Do you believe it's important to stand your ground and set boundaries, or do you believe it's important to soften and forgive others and yourself? Yes. Yes, yes, yes... It's all "yes, and"—not "either or."

Then we turned to a more complicated subject: the death of her partner, Rayya Elias, the year before. By way of catch-up, if Liz has not been on your radar since *Eat, Pray, Love*, she ended up eventually leaving the beautiful Brazilian man with whom she so famously fell in love in Bali, for Rayya. A Syrian writer, musician, and filmmaker, she had been Liz's best friend for years, and when Rayya was suddenly diagnosed with terminal cancer, Liz's life came to a screeching halt. She realized that not only was she in love with her friend, but she couldn't let her die without revealing, and celebrating, this new dimension of her devotion.

In her signature openness, Liz had written a social media post announcing this life shift that demonstrated in a powerful way how sexual preference should really be about loving who we love instead of choosing a team for life. But if Liz was unconventional, she seemed pretty mainstream compared to Rayya, whom she described wryly as a former "heroin speedball addict." Liz had romanticized the peaceful death she would help Rayya navigate, but it was not to be. As Liz describes it, Rayya's death was consistent with her life: tumultuous, wild, and unpredictable. In describing this intimate chapter, Elizabeth Gilbert unwittingly launched a new one for me.

"Was Rayya badass and powerful and fearless...or was she terrified, and angry, and shattered?" Liz asked me rhetorically, "Yes. The answer is yes to all of that. And I saw all of it from the front row." Then she turned that same paradoxical perspective on herself: "And was I a perfect, selfless, loving, adoring caregiver...or was I also trapped in my own need, and narcissism, and pain, and demands? Yes. Yes I was."

I walked away from our conversation contemplating compassion in a whole new way. And this led me to an important realization: I couldn't stop obsessing about the judgement of others until I stopped judging myself. It also made me take a broader view of what *my self* is. I am a human paradox! My life—in and out of the spotlight—has proven that I'm weak and strong, patient and impatient, brave and terrified, confident and insecure, generous and greedy, friendly and standoffish, lazy and motivated, dorky and stylish, loud and quiet, imperfect and perfect. I'm all of it. And that's okay. Like so much of what I've learned on this dig of self-discovery, this realization brought me to the understanding that I'm just like most everybody else. And yet, I'm not like anyone else. Yes and yes. None of us is just one thing. And the more we can learn to accept contradiction in others, the more we can turn down the dial on our own self-judgement.

BECOMING

"An existing individual is constantly in process of becoming..."
—Søren Kierkegaard

The idea of meeting myself with understanding and acceptance was pivotal. As the humanistic psychologist Carl Rogers says in his book *On Becoming a Person: A Therapist's View of Psychotherapy*, "The curious paradox is that when I accept myself just as I am, then I can change." Rogers differentiated between the real self and the ideal self—or, as I think of it, the real self and the mask we show to the world—and framed self-actualization as eliminating the gap between the two. In the book he refers to a client's "moving away from the compelling image of what he ought to be," as laid out by his parents in childhood. Put another way, abandoning the *self* he'd constructed for the purpose of procuring approval and love. In a way, his client was walking away from a life controlled by "should," graduating from Showing Off to Showing UP. Leaving behind a life designed to make everyone else comfortable means adopting a willingness to sometimes make them uncomfortable. For a people pleaser, this translates into learning to please yourself. And, like the practice of presence itself, it's a journey.

Consider how Michelle Obama explains the title of her extraordinary book, *Becoming*: "For me, becoming isn't about arriving somewhere or achieving a certain aim. I see it instead as forward motion, a means of evolving, a way to reach continuously toward a better self. The journey doesn't end." And here is what Abraham Maslow, the American psychologist who famously coined the "human hierarchy of needs," observed about self-actualizing people in his 1954 book *Motivation and Personality*: "Their ease of penetration to reality, their closer approach to an animal-like or child-like acceptance and spontaneity imply superior awareness of their own impulses, their own desires, opinions, and subjective reactions in general."

Another word for this is "equanimity." It's defined as *maintaining mental calmness, composure, and evenness of temper, especially in a difficult situation.* While I'm not claiming to have arrived at this lofty state, it's the goal towards which I am progressing. It's the *process* of my life, the practice. Like the winding route of the labyrinth, my path is circuitous, but I walk it with determination and appreciation. The movement toward acceptance of, rather than resistance to, reality means I can embrace life more fully— and that includes embracing any perceived flaws in myself, the idiosyncrasies and offenses of others, and whatever happens to be unfolding in the present moment. This requires repeatedly stepping away from the stories that are the stones in my ego castle, and recognizing that when a particular story holds emotion, that's a bread crumb leading me down another path, letting me know I have some work to do. Like a clue in an unfolding investigation, it's an indication that I need to pay attention. By breathing through it, by embodying it, I liberate this emotion from my cells, and from my soul. And then...acceleration ensues.

———————

Walking along the beach today, I had a profound experience of these practices enmeshed. As often happens when I'm in nature, poems arrived. Like childbirth, I am not in control of the timing. This time, it was a couple of lines I'd written the year before. They dropped into my head, and then suddenly demanded to be expanded upon. Like a sibling who arrives and completes the family.

Prompted by a close friend's story of a troubling relationship from her teenage years, these words had emerged:

I'm not too much
I'm too much for you

Today, as I walked by the ocean, they surfaced in my mind like a drowning person breaking through the surface of the water. Then the next two lines, gasping for air:

I'm so much
more than you can handle

I felt the impact at a soul level. I kept repeating it so as not to forget. I wanted to be able to write it down once I returned to the cottage. But slowly, I realized that every time I said the first line, I felt a small swell of emotion. So I started saying that line alone, over and over. *I'm not too much. I'm not too much. I'm not too much.* And I started to cry.

Dig, Nancy. Keep digging. Don't run away from this.

I'm not too much.

Pay dirt.

And here's the pay*off*: by the time I had reached the end of the sand, my recitation of the line had changed dramatically. I was no longer the wounded child I had been a few minutes before. I was a woman, owning the words, walking with a spring in my step and light in my eyes. That's my definition of transformation.

I'm not too much
I'm too much for you
I'm so much
more than you can handle.

LIGHT

―――――――――

*"If everything around you seems dark,
look again, you may be the light."*

—Rumi

Imagine you've been wrongly imprisoned for decades, but through ingenuity, determination, and hard work, you've dug a tunnel—à la *Shawshank Redemption*—from your jail cell to the roadside. Now, imagine the extraordinary sense of relief you'd feel as you broke through the last few inches of dirt to see the sunshine and blue sky. Emerging from the hole, you'd find yourself feeling markedly different than you did before—no longer trapped, but free; no longer fearful, but joyful; no longer defeated, but excited. The end of my tunnel expedition was as transformative as that— as if it were a birth canal. And as it happened, Dr. Wayne Dyer reached in and pulled me out with a pair of metaphysical forceps.

I had been aware of Dr. Dyer for years (mainly as the bald guy on PBS) and had been drawn in a couple of times by his TV presence, but I had never read his books. According to the legacy tribute PBS created, *The Forever Wisdom of Dr. Wayne Dyer*, over eighteen years Wayne reached millions of viewers through his outrageously popular broadcasts. Now here I was, in 2015, about to work with him. Introducing him and my friend Anne to audiences on his east coast tour. I had no idea how life-changing it would be.

I read Wayne's last book, first. He had just published *I Can See Clearly Now*, and it was a great starting point because it told his life story while imparting his current philosophy. I devoured it before our first show, in Montreal. The book includes a poignant description of Wayne standing at his father's grave. In that moment, he allowed himself to let go of the hatred and resentment he had harboured for a lifetime toward a father who had abandoned his family. Forgiveness was Wayne's ticket out of his own torture. Immediately afterwards, he checked into a little place called the Spindrift Motel and wrote his first self-help book, *Your Erroneous Zones*, in fourteen days. It became an international bestseller.

Meeting Wayne backstage before the shows was one thing. He was the most unassuming, gentle man. I particularly loved seeing the special relationship he had with Anne and Paul's kids. But after my part was done, I was able to sit and watch Wayne in action on stage. In fact, *action* is the wrong word. For the most part, he just sat in an armchair. He didn't need any fancy footwork or bells and whistles...because he was deeply present. He spoke for almost three hours, engaged in a one-way conversation with the audience, and you could've heard a pin drop in the place—except when we laughed, and there was a lot of that going on. Wayne was surprisingly funny, and the humour sprang from his recognition of the universal truths of human experience.

A master storyteller, Wayne played the crowd like a violin. Peppered through his talk were anecdotes, poems, and snippets of ancient wisdom. He always had an orange on a small table next to his chair and at some point in the evening, he would pick it up and ask the audience what would happen if he squeezed the orange as hard as he could. A few voices would respond from the crowd that juice would come out of it. "What kind of juice?" he'd ask. There'd be ripples of laughter, but someone would yell out the obvious answer: "Orange juice!" Then Wayne would take it to the next level: "*Why* will orange juice come out of this if I squeeze it?" After a pause, he'd deliver the answer. "Orange juice comes out of it because that's what's inside it. And human beings are the same: when we get squeezed, what comes out of us is what's inside of us."

I had made a similar observation a few months before, after driving my daughter to school during a bad winter storm. When I came home, I announced to my husband that I had come to a significant conclusion: under pressure, nice people get nicer and cranky people get crankier. I love how a simple analogy can trigger a profound cascade of self-awareness. When I was squeezed by stress, fear, or frustration, anger poured out. But listening to Wayne speak, orange in hand, I considered for the first time that these emotions—the ones I'd never embodied—were trapped inside of me instead of just moving through. It was like a light had switched on in me (how apt that Wayne's tour was called I Am Light) but the light bulb didn't go on in my head…it lit up my heart and soul.

Driving home from our second show in Moncton, I felt "lighter" than I had in years. As I navigated the highway, music blasting, I felt transported into a whole new mindset. I realized that if we are all indeed filled with light, as Wayne insisted, then I had been hiding mine for a long time, not only from everyone else, but also from myself. All of a sudden, I pictured the dimmer switch in the living room of my childhood home. As a kid, I was fascinated that you could turn the dial all the way down without clicking it off, but it would *appear* that the pot lights in the ceiling were out. *That's me*, I thought as I drove along the highway. *My inner light's been turned down for so long, I forgot I had one.* And in that moment of pure presence, I knew it was finally time to do something about it. Time to take control of my dimmer switch. Part of the power of this new perspective was recognizing that despite all my years standing in a spotlight, external approval and attention had not lit me up. It couldn't. It felt good while it lasted, but its warmth was never sustainable because I didn't feel my own light.

I didn't feel my own light.

This was a huge personal realization, but it had professional ramifications as well. At the time I was discovering, through my presentation training, how much I loved helping others, and it gave me a broader and deeper understanding of the fear of public speaking. After that, my career path took a turn for the subversively soulful. I mean, sure, I can give you tips, tricks, and techniques to be a better presenter, but you'll never really be comfortable on stage until you find a way to befriend fear—particularly that fear of not being enough. So, the Dimmer Theory became a fundamental principle of my work with clients.

Here's how I see it. We are all born with our lights ablaze. You only need to observe babies and toddlers to witness this. They are completely without inhibition, unconcerned with anyone else's judgement or opinions. Then the messages start: *Don't be so loud; Don't take up too much space; Don't shine so brightly.* All those *Don't*s start to nudge the dimmer downwards. *Parenting as firefighting.* In defence of our mothers and fathers, though, as we touched on before, part of the reason they do this is it's the only parenting model they've ever known. It's also no doubt motivated by a desire to help their kids fit in with their peer group, and to make sure that they succeed rather than being excluded from things because of their "outstanding behaviour." Of course, there's another side to it, and it has a lot to do with ego.

Parents often see their children as reflections of themselves—like mini ambassadors. So, as we grow up, we learn that we're supposed to care *what the neighbours think.* We learn to turn our own dimmer down. Another factor: we don't want to be picked on, bullied, or teased, so the question becomes *How can I fit in?* And *How can I* not *stand out?* Then the teen years hit, and the dimmer takes another dive. Between the pressure imposed by others and our own self-consciousness, our light gets turned down so low, we forget it's there. All too often, it takes years—maybe even decades—to remember that light...and sadly, some people never reconnect to it.

Here's the other thing about my Dimmer Theory. If you eventually do find the switch, it's not as straightforward as simply turning it up to full brightness. It took time—and the judgement of others (and yourself)—to dim that light, and it will take time to turn it up again. Remember, this is a practice, so it's not a straightforward journey. Try to think of this as a project instead of a problem. That way, you can give yourself permission to slip two steps backward after gaining ground.

A couple of weeks after our tour, Anne and I flew to Hawaii for a writers' workshop hosted by Wayne. It was a short but transformative trip. Anne had become close friends with Wayne and he now treated her more like a daughter than a producer. We had dinner with him two nights in a row, and I became utterly convinced that Wayne Dyer was the real deal. It's probably not a surprise that someone as fear-based as me is skeptical by nature. I had met enough famous people by then to know I wasn't the only one walking through life with a mask, so I was tickled pink to have the chance to spend time with this brilliant teacher in his natural habitat. He loved Maui and Kaanapali Beach, and it was in his home there that he would die suddenly two months later.

Like many of his fans and followers around the world, I was devastated to hear of his passing. But I will always treasure the time I spent in his company, and I'll be forever grateful for the role he played in my life. Like a divine electrician, he reconnected me to my light—by helping me *see clearly* the layers of filters I had been hiding behind and identifying the erroneous thought patterns that had kept me in the dark for so long.

Wayne communicated a lot of wisdom through his books, often serving up ancient philosophy for modern audiences. But that workshop also got *me* writing in a whole new way, enabling me to allow my innermost thoughts and feelings to surface on the page. This is the magic of journalling, and I highly recommend it as a method to reconnect you to your own light. Here's an example of a writing prompt we were given one afternoon at that retreat. It was simply this: *The one thing you need to know about me is...* Here's the answer I wrote that day:

> *...that I feel right now like I'm being born. I have lived my*
> *whole life in the shadows of lack of worthiness, while others*
> *constantly shone a light on me. They told me I was special,*
> *but I never bought it. I felt like a fraud who had the world*
> *fooled. I am just now coming out of the birth canal into the*
> *Light of Love (as the song goes). Seeing myself for the first time*
> *with kind and compassionate eyes. Not "special" in the way*
> *that my TV viewers held me because of celebrity, but beautiful*
> *in my sameness and oneness with others. Perfectly imperfect.*
> *Imperfectly perfect.*

Lesley also confused me. We first met when I interviewed her for a series of newspaper articles I was writing on the top twenty-five people changing the face of our city. My perception of her was as a high-powered businessperson, specializing in corporate leadership, but as I discovered when I entered her "office," she was also a wild, open, and creative spirit. And she was entirely comfortable talking about spiritual matters. She even had a small personal altar in her workspace, complete with a meditation cushion. As it turned out, she was one of eight highly successful individuals on that list who disclosed a regular reliance on meditation. This was both a shock to my system and, unknowingly, a glimpse into my future.

When I first encountered Louise Hay's work, I was still pretty armoured up. I was intrigued, but I wasn't ready to metabolize her philosophy of self-love. To live it. The idea did catch something in me, though, like a hook in the mouth of a fish. I wasn't ready to be reeled in yet, but I was on my way—whether I knew it or not. At first, I could only digest Louise's approach in very small doses. Her prescribed "mirror work" was beyond me. Looking into a mirror and saying things to myself like *"I love and accept you"*; *"You are wonderful"*; *"You are worthy of love"* made my skin crawl. I physically could not utter these statements. But even my reticence showed me there was something to this. *Why* couldn't I do it? What was it about seeing myself with love that was so repulsive to me? So, I started to listen to Louise's recordings. Like television's Mr. Rogers, she had a disconcertingly slow cadence to her speech. But she wasn't speaking to my mind; her communication was directed at my soul. And eventually, the message got through. I'll always be grateful to this supremely loving woman for helping to unlock my suit of armour. And she did that for people all over the world by devoting herself to helping us move from loathing to loving, and building an esteem-powered publishing house, Hay House, for authors like Wayne Dyer.

"Self-love" is a funny term. For a long time, I couldn't even say the phrase without feeling completely goofy. But now I understand why. I was living in a realm called "self-loathing," which is so far removed from self-love it seems unreachable. If you ever stop and ask for directions in New England and the explanation is overly complicated, there's an old saying you might hear: "You can't get there from here." That's how I felt about self-love. When I discovered my own light and figured out that I had control of the dimmer switch, it still took me a while to adjust the brightness. To some extent, I had to retrace my journey, driving back through *like* to arrive at *love*. If you're contemplating this soulful road trip, I suggest patience and persistence. I believe awakening to this light is a gradual process—even if it seems to arrive in a flash.

My own conversation with Oprah more than twenty years ago— the one I brought up earlier when we were talking about our masks—played a part in my eventual understanding of the light within. The TV time slots for Oprah and *Live at 5* were back-to-back. Her four o'clock show was the lead-in for ours, bridging the audience from afternoon soap opera fare. Then our program, a newsmagazine, did the same for the harder news package at six o'clock. All this to say that luckily for me, we were able to secure a sit-down interview with Oprah because of this affiliate relationship.

I flew to Chicago with a videographer for a two-day trip, and it was the first time I had a date with a major celebrity without being overcome by nerves. I attended a double-show taping the first day, and then had my interview the second. Just being at Harpo

Studios was a thrill. Oprah wasn't just my lead-in; she was a role model and an inspiration. In some ways, I had been imitating her for years with my fake-it-till-you-make-it approach. I loved watching her in action that first day—observing how she handled herself when the tape was rolling, and when it wasn't. She was funny, self-deprecating, and real. And her audience adored her.

The next morning, when I was led back into the studio, I realized I'd be sitting with Oprah on her set, asking the questions! Mind officially blown. She was immediately relaxed and familiar. In fact, she quickly took to calling me Nance—a term of endearment typically used only by my close friends. During the course of our conversation, I got around to asking her about the extraordinary wealth she was accumulating. I knew she came from a poor and abusive childhood and wondered if she ever felt guilty about her money. She replied without hesitation, "Hell no! I never understood that. I mean, if you worked hard and earned it, why should you feel guilty?!" But she added a caveat that would stay with me for the rest of my life: "I do believe—as the saying goes—'From those to whom much is given, much is expected.'" I didn't know at the time this was a biblical reference, but those words wrapped around me and embedded themselves in my psyche. In some ways, they're the foundation of my belief that when we stay anchored in a sense of contribution rather than performance—when we Show UP instead of Showing Off—our life expands. *Thanks, Ope!*

SHARING LIGHT

I remember the first time I saw my friend Anne do a Facebook Live video. It was my introduction to the possibility of truly Showing UP. She had no notes, no slides, and—this was the revolutionary part—she just talked. To tell the truth, at first I found myself cringing a bit. It wasn't polished; it certainly wasn't perfect. But very quickly, this sense of awe came over me, because she was so damn comfortable. She was genuine and relaxed, and that quickly made up for any rough edges in her performance. In fact, the sheer beauty in it was that she wasn't "performing" at all.

This experience was an inspiration for my next chapter. I was finally starting to feel my own light, and I was ready to share it. I had also evolved into a greater comfort with embracing the light in others. This first took the form of a podcast I started out of the blue, with no sponsors and no help, called *The Soul Booth*. It was 2017, and Donald Trump had recently won the American election. There seemed to be so much turmoil and hate in the world, and yet I constantly found myself meeting and having rich conversations with beautiful people; individuals whose contributions to our world were rooted in love. So, I decided it was my responsibility to put my broadcasting background to good use and start sharing those voices. My intentions are best captured by a favourite quote of mine by Edith Wharton: "There are two ways of spreading light: to be the candle or the mirror that reflects it." My guests would be the candles, and I'd reflect their stories, sharing their light with as many people as I could. But I would also commit to sharing my own flame—with no filter.

One of the brightest candles I've ever known was my friend Audrey Parker. Her journey was a dynamic example of how meaningful and transformative a deep sense of contribution can be in our lives, and she shared that powerfully in a video recording of *The Soul Booth*. Audrey's breast cancer had already metastasized to her skeleton by the time she was diagnosed, but she immediately took the news in stride. In fact, waiting for the results of a CT scan that day in February of 2016, this dynamo of a woman announced with determination: "Whatever they tell me, I'm going to be joyful. If they tell me I don't have cancer, I'm going to be joyful. If they tell me I'm dying, I'm going to be joyful. I'm not going to waste a minute of my time feeling sorry for myself." Now, it's one thing to make that kind of pronouncement and quite another to follow through. But that's exactly what Audrey did, and it left everyone around her mesmerized. She celebrated every moment, delighting in her friendships and truly making her days count. In the two and a half years of her cancer journey, she taught everyone around her how to live by the way she was choosing to die, and people were drawn to her *light* like moths to a flame.

Two years after Audrey's cancer diagnosis, the insidious disease started to make its way into the lining of her brain. She knew it was probably only a matter of time before it interfered with her cognitive functioning. Audrey had been assessed and approved for Medical Assistance in Dying (MAID) and was passionately intent on maintaining control over the timing and circumstance of her death. I remember the day she found out that her approval for MAID wouldn't mean anything if she wasn't *compos mentis* ("of sound mind") at the time of the injections. She was extremely frustrated and disappointed. Our conversation is burned into my memory. I tried to comfort her by saying, "No, Aud, don't worry about that. We'll get a good lawyer and create a legal document to maintain your MAID no matter what happens." She answered with a sense of finality: "No, Nance, the law won't allow that. It's an open-and-shut case." That was one of the very few times I witnessed her feeling defeated.

However, reopening that case became Audrey's life's purpose—and, as it turns out, her *cause célèbre*. You often hear of people fighting for their lives, but Aud was fighting for her death. It wasn't all about her, though. Throughout her illness, she used the platform her very public fight had given her to preach kindness. Her motto was "Be kind because you can," and she embodied that approach. Her departure was the ultimate act of kindness. She *left* before she had to for two reasons: to draw attention to the fact that people who are assessed and approved for MAID (and who are not considered vulnerable—that's important!) should not be precluded from their medically assisted death if they lose cognitive capacity before scheduled injections; and, on a personal level, to be sure she would experience the kind of death she wanted.

Aud's sense of contribution was a saving grace at the end of her life. She became a national media darling, and people across Canada reached out to express their gratitude, to let her know how much she'd inspired them. At a gathering of her closest friends shortly before her *departure date*, Audrey stood in the centre of the room, radiating love, and offered her own expression of gratitude: "Finally, I would like to thank everyone who has filled my life with joy and love the past two and a half years. By supporting me, you have made it possible for me to use my story to help others. It has been one of the most satisfying experiences of all my life." Audrey's amendment, as it became known, passed into law as part of Bill C-7 in the spring of 2021, a year and a half after her own passing. As a result, late-stage consent can now be waived under specific circumstance's like Aud's, in which a person has been "assessed and approved" for MAID, and is at risk of losing decision-making capacity before their scheduled death.

Audrey was always teaching those around her, and I was one of her devoted students. But she was hungry to learn as well. She loved the fact that I was on a spiritual path—a "seeker," as she described me—and would often quiz me about what I was reading or thinking about. It was also a source of bemusement to her that I could have done so well professionally while harbouring such insecurity. One day, she announced that I had a lot in common with Princess Di. I looked at her in astonishment. I mean, seriously? Was I *really* going to have the audacity to compare myself to Diana, Princess of Wales?! She is perhaps the most globally beloved figure in recent history. So, in some ways, this next section makes my skin crawl. But yes, I'm going to go way out on a limb and draw some parallels. And chances are, you might recognize yourself in parts of this narrative as well.

It is widely documented that Diana Spencer grew up with a gnawing insecurity, and yet as a teenager she portrayed a sense of confidence. She came from a well-to-do family, carried herself with poise, and was well-versed in social graces. She was a quirky child who loved acting, but as she grew into a "pretty" teenager, the world took notice of her appearance. In particular, the Prince of Wales. Diana stepped into the most public of lives, as a member of the royal family, and had a love-hate relationship with the spotlight, because while the attention served to light her up in a way she had long desired, I believe it also may have constantly reminded her that (in her own mind) she didn't deserve the adulation. I think of it as a dichotomy of confidence: a delicate balance of self-hatred and narcissism.

I can relate to so much of that. Even the part about wanting a prince to come and save me. But in the end, as Diana and I both learned the hard way, we can only save ourselves. I do believe that other people play vital roles in our personal evolution, though. Often when we can't seem to get the love we desperately want from others, it can actually serve us profoundly by leading us to the realization that the love we need most lies within us.

When Elton John sang "Goodbye England's Rose" to the tune of "Candle in the Wind" at Princess Diana's funeral, it was a heartbreaking tribute to her contribution to the world. She did so much for so many, but I think her humanitarian work also served as a path out of her own insecurity. I would argue that her evolution from *Princess Di* to *Diana* was one from ingenue to empowered, mature woman, and that it happened not in spite of her pain and suffering, but *because* of it. Looking back, it seems like she was really just stepping into herself, feeling her own light and amplifying it through the meaningful work she was doing in the world. Even her physical body reflected her growth. After years of bulimia and the resulting waif-like body, photos from the final summer of her life show that she had a new fullness to her figure. She looked healthy. A visual representation of how Diana had grown into herself.

I'm fifty-five now, and when thoughts about my body being larger than it once was (I definitely gained the COVID-19!) swirl around my head, I snatch these thoughts in mid-air and flick them very intentionally with my middle finger right into orbit. Super satisfying. Then I quickly replace them with these words: *I am more of myself than ever.* Sometimes I employ my punny sense of humour and issue a reminder: *I matter more.* I do matter more...to me.

Once in a while I feel like saying to myself, "Oh, *there* you are!" It's like the little girl in me—authentic, fun-loving, oblivious to others' opinions—was waiting a long time for permission to re-emerge. *Fancy Nancy.*

This is far from a unique experience, and I am always fortified by hearing other women talk about this transition. Jann Arden, singer, songwriter, TV star, wrote beautifully about this in her book *If I Knew Then: Finding Wisdom in Failure and Power in Aging* in a section about how she hopes she will one day look at the older version of herself in the mirror: "I will love that old woman ferociously," she says, "because she has finally figured out how to live a life of purpose—not in spite of but because of all her mistakes and failures."

When I think back to my constantly shifting hairstyles on *Live at 5*, I see a lot of symbolism in my various 'do's (and don'ts!). I was never happy with my appearance for long, and it was so attached to my search for validation. At fifty, I took that symbolism into my own hands and stepped out of the struggle. I stopped wrestling with the grey roots that stubbornly appeared every two weeks and decided to *accept* them. Over the course of a summer, I grew my hair out and then cropped it super short. It was probably the most liberating thing I've ever done. For the first time I could remember, I didn't have to colour or style my hair. Fresh out of the shower, I would run my fingers through it once with some product, and I'd be done. But much more significantly, I was breaking free of the opinions of others. And Showing UP as the silver-haired fifty-year-old I was. This wasn't a judgement of anyone else's choices. This was all about me, accepting myself, both inside and out. And you know what? I realized something: I'm not an old grey mare, I'm a silver fox! Even if I need to remind myself of this at times.

REMOVING THE MASK & FANNING THE FLAME

It's hard to take off the mask once you've worn it for so long, but the conditions also have to be ripe for its lowering. I still find myself donning my mask when I don't feel safe. When I'm with someone with whom I don't feel energetically in tune, my natural instinct is to raise the walls of protection. It's easiest to Show UP in the company of people you feel truly seen by (and those aren't always the ones closest to you), but this is only the beginning. The greater challenge is to take this new authenticity into the deep end of the pool, where it's more crowded and you have to either swim or tread water. No standing safely in the shallow end. Being real in a fake world.

My mask has a lot to do with my ego. In fact, ego was the conductor in my symphony of Showing Off. However, I want to clarify again my meaning when I use the word "ego": I'm not equating it with vanity, as in, "Oh, that person has an enormous ego!" which might suggest that he or she is conceited or thinks too highly of themselves. Conversely, in my experience, an inflated ego is often a sign of a deflated sense of self-worth.

Learning to love myself was not what I expected. It wasn't about looking on the bright side or trying to remain focussed on my positive attributes, but actually *embracing* all parts of myself— unconditionally. Growing up, "self-centred" was one of the worst things you could call someone. It was clearly derogatory, but when you step back and consider it, the irony is obvious. It's evidence of the way we learned, as we grew, to negate ourselves. To celebrate others' achievements, talents, and successes, but never our own. Shouldn't we all aim to be self-*centred*? You can't step fully into your purpose if you're hiding your light under a bushel. What I now know is that embracing our inner light is like plugging into a power source—it connects us to the current of the world in a meaningful way, allowing us more opportunities to contribute, converse, and share, and that in turn lights us up further. And contribution is a lot more potent when it stems from a sense of our own worthiness rather than a need for recognition. I struggled with writing this book for that very reason. Writing a memoir feels like a very self-centred act, and I had to constantly remind myself that I had something worthy of sharing, and that the focus was on helping others rather than impressing them.

Learning to embrace my own light and creating a new habit of Showing UP meant I had to learn to be full of myself.

> *Conceited*
> *is a conceit*
> *Be full of yourself, I say*
> *Feel your goodness*
> *Revel in your talents*
> *Value your self*
> *Stand your ground*

I read Anita Moorjani's book *Dying to Be Me* on that trip from Halifax to Hawaii just after the tour with Wayne Dyer. I was moved by its persuasive message about loving ourselves. The subtitle, *My Journey from Cancer to Near Death to True Healing*, tells the story in brief. As Anita describes, she believes she got sick with cancer because she had always focused on taking care of everyone's needs but her own, and her fear and self-doubt manifested physically. Her near-death experience showed her a new way of living; one in which she feels a "soul-deep sense of self-love." When she awakened in the hospital after clinically dying, she knew she was going to survive, and in the next few weeks experienced a spontaneous remission. She went from lying in a hospital bed in a coma with organs failing, to vibrant health in a shockingly short period of time, and her scans are proof of this miraculous recovery.

Her mission now is to convince the rest of us we deserve our own love. "We are born perfect," she says, "but spend a lifetime trying to be something we are not, and then feel inadequate for failing. Your only purpose is to be yourself, otherwise you will deprive the Universe of who you came here to be." Those words really impacted me, and I wrote in my notebook while still airborne, *I feel a bizarre gratitude for Anita sharing her journey; almost like—because she died in order to learn the lesson, I don't have to.*

Little did I know that I would work with Anita less than a year later. Anne and Paul were bringing her to Halifax for a day-long workshop, and it was my job to welcome the crowd and be a stage presence throughout the day, weaving the different elements of the program together. The evening before, I found myself frantic with worry. I hadn't prepared anything. No script, no notes, no thoughts. This was totally unlike me. Being prepared was my *thang*, my security blanket. But when GUS started nagging me that night about getting to work on some ideas to help me be clever and charming the next day, I did something entirely new. I took a breath, and unexpectedly gave birth to the title of this book: "Nope," I said to my friend fear, "I'm not Showing Off tomorrow, I'm just going to Show UP." And that is just what I did.

It should be noted that I *showed up* in sparkly shoes. Dressing myself has always been a challenge because of something lurking in my closet: perfectionism. My insecurity means that before an event, I often change countless times to get it just right. Perhaps a hangover from my time on television, I still worry about looking the part I've been asked to play. It's also about looking good, but not too good—not shining too much. That morning, I went to grab a pair of shoes that matched my outfit and gravitated to the obvious choice. But a fun, glittery silver pair of flats caught my eye. I had bought them years before but never worn them. As I went rogue and reached for them, GUS had a little hissy fit: "Are you crazy?! You can't wear those!" That was the sign I needed to convince me that they were the right choice. I was about to reclaim *Fancy Nancy*.

I told the story of that morning's footwear selection during my introduction, and in doing so, I shared more of myself than ever. I was relaxed, excited about the day, and utterly in the moment. It was the first time on stage when fear was tucked snugly in my back pocket, and you know what? I was good, because I was present. And I was focused on my *contribution*.

When I ran into Paul in the registration area during our mid-morning break, he looked at me with a smile of recognition. "I've never seen you like that on stage before. You showed them your full self. You're on fire." By this time, Paul and I had worked on many events together, and he had seen me perform in a variety of settings and contexts. But he had never seen me Show UP publicly without my mask. His comments that day served as confirmation I was on the right path, and that I needed to follow this trajectory—allowing my true self to sparkle, just like my shoes.

CREATING SPARKS

"Connection is the energy that exists between people when they feel seen, heard, and valued; when they can give and receive without judgement, and when they derive sustenance and strength from the relationship."
—Brené Brown, *The Gifts of Imperfection*

In her oft-quoted poem, "Our Greatest Fear," author and spiritual leader Marianne Williamson writes, "It is our light not our darkness that most frightens us," poignantly describing our reluctance to allow ourselves to shine. I encourage you to search out this poem on the internet, and don't just read it—print it out or copy it in your own hand and post it where you can see it every day! This powerful poem ends with the conclusion that our willingness to shine our light demonstrates to others that it's okay to shine theirs too, and that as we liberate ourselves from fear, our resulting freedom frees others.

This brings to mind the word "namaste." Though derived from ancient Sanskrit, you'll hear it a lot in the western world today—particularly in yoga studios. A respectful Hindu greeting still used in India and Nepal, it's a beautiful salutation that communicates reverence. There are variations in translation, but the one I love is, "The light in me honours the light in you." Feeling my own light has enabled to appreciate the light in others. Seeing others shine no longer feels like a threat to me. It's reason to celebrate.

I'm happy to report that this recognition has significantly expanded and deepened my relationships. Where I had long allowed fear to inhibit my friendships with other women, I'm now blessed with a bevy of beautiful souls who love me unconditionally, and the feeling is mutual. I'm a huge fan of the Canadian novelist Donna Morrissey, and was fortunate enough a few years ago to take a writing course with her. In her new memoir, *Pluck,* Donna includes this gorgeous passage about the transformative nature of female friendship:

They are the caregivers of our hearts....They seek treasures from the dark and create structure out of chaos and chase the she-devil victim from our stoop. Their instruments are acceptance and understanding and they shield us with love.

The wondrous part of authentic relationships like this is that they also teach you how to strengthen your connection to yourself.

"Run to the rescue with love, and peace will follow." This line was offered by Joaquin Phoenix in his acceptance speech when he won the 2020 Oscar for Best Actor for his role in the film *Joker.* The words were lyrics from a song written by his brother River, who at age twenty-three, in the midst of a tremendously successful movie career, died of a drug overdose. I saw a clip of Joaquin's acceptance speech while I was writing this book, and it immediately spoke to me. The line may have been about showing compassion to others (as River was a committed humanitarian), but to me, it's particularly poignant when applied to self-love. You know all that kindness, empathy, and compassion you show others? You deserve it too! Give it to yourself. You want to be cherished? You must lead the way. Think of the golden rule—treat others how you wish to be treated—and turn it inward: treat *yourself* how you want others to treat you. Start there.

Elizabeth Gilbert appears to have this relationship with love figured out. During our podcast recording, she told me about the most amazing love letters she's ever received—not from either of her ex-husbands, not from Rayya, but from love itself. As she famously revealed in *Eat, Pray, Love,* the author suffered a depression that lasted almost three years. "There was so much that I didn't know about how to take care of my own heart and my own fragile-ness then and all I knew how to do was to collapse into shame and despair." She described throwing every possible solution at the problem with no success, until something magical happened. Remember our letters from fear? Liz started writing letters from love.

I do remember one night...in the middle of a long string of nights of just horrified panic, being awake and unable to calm myself—wishing that somebody would calm me, wishing that there was somebody who would just fix it. I remember just thinking, *What if I were to write myself a letter, saying everything I wish somebody would say to me?* And so I wrote that letter, and it was the most incredible, loving thing I'd ever created. And it was 'I love you. You're perfect. I've got you...' and even though I had never heard those words, I managed to find them. That's grace.

This creative practice of self-love has served Liz well; over the past two decades, she's written hundreds of thousands of pages. She calls it a conversation between her "brokenness" and love. And the sharing of the practice has helped countless others—myself included. During our interview, I mentioned to Liz that I had been inspired by a poem she had shared in her book *Big Magic*. It was actually written by another Gilbert: Jack Gilbert (no relation) was a poet whom Liz has referred to as the poet laureate of her life. This excerpt from "A Brief for the Defense" is about finding light in the darkness:

> We must risk delight. We can do without pleasure,
> but not delight. Not enjoyment. We must have
> the stubbornness to accept our gladness in the ruthless
> furnace of this world.

I told Liz I had been thinking about this excerpt ever since I'd read it, and that it had helped shape my new, less guarded approach to life. As I put it, "No matter where you go, no matter what energy you're met with, if you are stubbornly friendly and just reach out with love, it's amazing what you get back." Liz Gilbert looked at me, smiled, and replied, "And can you imagine doing that if you're the only person in the room?"

I was speechless.

Self-friendliness is an invaluable perspective. When I was allowing my inner critic to run roughshod over me, I was treating myself in a way I'd never treat a friend. And for that matter, if a friend treated me that way, we wouldn't be friends for long! Being stubbornly friendly to myself means more than being compassionate and supportive. It means drawing a sacred circle around myself to create boundaries. This is a very different form of protection than my old castle constructed by ego and patrolled by fear. Instead of leaving me feeling weak and isolated, my new boundaries empower me. They're drawn where they suit *me*, not others—because I'm worth it. And when I honour those boundaries, I can move through the world feeling safe and strong.

Part of this new paradigm has been learning how to say no to others. Kindly, but firmly. Loving myself has reconnected me to my inner wisdom—my instinct and intuition. That same force that got me up out of my grade-4 chair the day Mrs. W tried to dim my light. It's also enabled me to look back at my younger self with kindness, and even admiration. I don't have to rely on my imagination for this, because I've got hundreds of hours of tape and seemingly endless clips on YouTube! Knowing the psychological challenges I faced as a television host, it's heartening now to be bear witness to my courage and my character.

One of these special memories captured on video was a series I did about a man named Michael DeCourciere. He was dying in a newly established AIDS hospice. A team of thirty people (some friends, some strangers) had formed to provide around-the-clock care, and I was there to shed some light on the subject. It was a time when not much was known about the disease and there was a lot of fear and stigma around it. I have a visceral memory from my first visit, of being offered a cup of tea. The fact that I was initially nervous about using the cup speaks volumes. However, as is so often the case with fear, mine was born of ignorance, and my exposure to this new situation expanded my world. I eventually got so comfortable that I sat on Michael's bed with him, talking and laughing, and I knew it was significant for my viewers to see me in such an intimate setting with this human being. He was a beautiful man, and the whole experience taught me a lot about love.

The light in me honours the light in you.

It's essential for me to say that this is a practice; it requires vigilance to prevent myself from slipping back into old habits. The meaning of the word "failure" has morphed dramatically for me over the years. It used to mean the possibility of people not liking me, judging me as unintelligent, thinking I'm not nice. Can you see the irony here? Success, for me, used to mean donning my mask so well no one ever knew I was wearing it. Now, it means sharing my true face, regardless of whether people like it or not. I'm not here to put my integrity aside or pretend to be something I'm not to reap approval or praise. To sell out. To Show Off. But my response to this *new* form of failure is also very different. I catch myself, and then instead of criticizing, I coach. Like my best basketball coaches, I am gentle but focused, expressly guiding myself away from destructive habits and encouraging constructive ones.

According to the work of the celebrated American psychologist Dr. John Gottman, successful relationships should have a ratio of five positive interactions for every negative one—what he calls "the magic ratio." If you turn that lens on your relationship with yourself, you might quickly realize that ratio is reversed. The biggest lesson I've learned is that when we stop worrying about our inadequacies and legitimately recognize our own goodness, we come to the startling and liberating realization that we really are enough. And then, the world opens up to us.

———————

Ten months before Louise Hay transitioned out of this life, her Hay House team threw her a ninetieth birthday bash. The party was held in a large auditorium and included a who's who of her stable of famous authors. Also in attendance was a Canadian man who had written a song that was played that night. Paul Luftenegger's "My Heart" was chosen because of its alignment to Louise's heart meditation, in which she directed listeners as follows: "Put one hand on your heart and one hand on your belly. And as you breathe quietly, notice how comforting that feels. Be aware that you can do this anytime and anywhere and take care of yourself."

But Paul had no knowledge of Louise Hay when he composed the song. His own path had been carved by tragedy. After suffering the trauma of his father's death by suicide in 2011, Paul sold his dad's prized Triumph motorcycle and used the money to buy himself a piano and microphone. He set to work creating music that would heal—what he calls "conscious music." His intention for "My Heart" was for it to be not just a song, but a tool for self-love as well as a musical meditation. Somehow, a bestselling author stumbled upon the song years later and hatched the plan to have it played at Louise's birthday party.

As the music played that night, everyone in the room put their hands on their hearts. It was a moment of pure beauty.

But the song had already changed Paul's life. Once launched, "My Heart" sailed far and wide. Farther and wider than he ever could've envisioned. It earned him an international audience and opportunities to perform in countries around the world. The song is played in hospitals and hospices, anywhere there's healing work to be done. He's even performed three times at the United Nations Headquarters in New York City. So, this young man who was once a boy bullied for being gay, has reaped the rewards of learning to love himself.

Paul and his partner, Cori, were guests of mine on *The Canadian Love Map* podcast, and while we talked about their love story, the focus was also on Paul's purpose-driven music career. One of Louise's enduring messages is that we miss a huge opportunity with children; we teach them years of math but neglect to teach them how to value themselves. Part of Paul's mission is to change that for humans of all ages, and he's become a devotee of Louise's work, even coaching and conducting Heal Your Life workshops. His experience at Louise's big birthday party was life-changing, but another performance of the song, this time for a smaller crowd, would also take Paul's breath away.

Two teachers in Ottawa, Jacquie Knelsen and Michelle Fizzard, had become fans of Paul's heart-centred music and reached out to let him know they had been playing it all year for their elementary class. Paul decided to make a trip to the capital city, keyboard in tow, to surprise the kids. But he didn't know what was in store for him. He was surprised to walk into a diverse, multicultural classroom, many of the children recent Syrian refugees. When he sat down to play "My Heart" for them and sang the opening words, "Put your hand on your heart," all of these seven- and eight-year-olds gently placed their hands on their chests. Then they sang along. They knew all the words, and more importantly, they had absorbed their meaning.

Feel your breath
Beneath that beautiful heart
Yes, there's a beautiful heart
In your chest

Louise had left the world, but Paul was still delivering her love with every note he played and every word he sang. And he still is. I encourage you to listen to this song, in stillness, with your eyes closed. Feel your own beautiful heart.

My friend Audrey had a tough childhood, but her determination and positive energy helped her craft a life full of fun, travel, and friends. It wasn't without darkness, though. She went through her own tunnel journey and her end-of-life chapter turned out to be the brightest of her life. I was inspired to tears when she watched a video of a message she'd recorded for a local fundraising event. She was too sick to attend, but I shot video of it playing on the big screen and the adoring reaction of the audience. In the middle of watching her own little speech, she announced matter-of-factly, "I really like myself." It took my breath away. But my greatest lesson in self-love was in the moments before Aud's "departure." There were only a handful of us in the room, and it was a private and intimate experience. I am sharing this remembrance because I know Audrey would want me to.

How do you imagine the final moments of your life? Most of us don't like to think about it at all, and many of us imagine them filled with fear. Now, try this alternative on for size. You're lying propped up by pillows in your comfortable bed, surrounded by people who love you deeply. You've had the chance to tell them what they mean to you, and to hear their expressions of love and appreciation for you. You have been given the gift of a deep knowledge that your life has made a difference to others, and to the world. Your favourite musician has been singing softly and playing guitar just outside your room, and you call her in and ask her to play a certain song. It will be the last piece of music you will hear before the injections are administered and you gently transition out of this life. It sounds like a dream sequence, doesn't it? Well, this was the reality of Audrey Parker's last few moments on Earth, and it was just the way she dreamed it could be. She was free of fear, and full of gratitude. Joyful.

"My legs, they are a part of my body.
My eyes, they are a part of my soul..."

Audrey closed her eyes as Laura Smith sang these first two lines, and then she started to sing along. I sat on the bed, transfixed. I had not known what to expect during this experience, but I had been well counselled by wise friends. *"Allow whatever happens to happen." "Just be there for her." "Focus on the quality of your presence and stay in the moment no matter what."* But this moment stunned me, and I was consumed by one thought: *This is the most beautiful thing I have ever seen.*

As Aud sang along, it became apparent that she knew the words well, and that she felt them to her core.

"Look deep, look deep.
There's a surprise there.

There's a surprise there.
Such a surprise
I'm a beauty."

Her face was the picture of peace and her body was relaxed, but most mesmerizing was that in this moment, she was utterly alone. Although we surrounded her, she was not singing for us. Audrey Jane Parker was singing to herself, for herself. At the end of her long journey, she was truly coming home. And she was serene.

"My face, it's a map of my time here.
My heart, it's a map of my dreams.
Dream deep, dream deep.
There's a surprise there.
There's a surprise.
Such a surprise
I'm a beauty."

In a world where most of us cling to our masks to hide our insecurities and private anxieties, it is profoundly powerful to witness someone in this kind of moment, embracing themselves with such love and tenderness.

Aud said many times that she wanted people to change the way they look at death, to view their last breath as something that should be celebrated and honoured in the same way as their first. She never wavered from that stance, and when it came to the last moments of her time here, she got the peaceful death she fought for. And she left us all wrapped in her love.

So, here's an idea. How about we all accept this lesson from Audrey? Instead of committing to a list of ways in which we can improve our shortcomings, what if we make a pact with ourselves to practice seeing our own beauty and feeling our own light? It's kind of revolutionary, but Audrey would *love* the idea of her life and death inspiring you to fall in love with yourself. You can start by listening to "I'm a Beauty." Ideally, put on some headphones. Turn it up loud, drown out any negative self-talk, and really feel it. *Repeat* until you believe it! For now, I'll leave you with a poem I wrote in the week after Aud's death. I can feel her presence and gentle guidance in each line.

> *Letting go of my story*
> *Stripping off the old mask*
> *To let the peace in*
> *I just have to ask*
>
> > *I am a tap and the water runs through me*
> > *Saying goodbye to all those who knew me*
> > *Fear is an anchor and love is a buoy*
>
> *Don't have to struggle*
> *Don't have to try*
> *Accept and allow*
> *No more wrestling with Why*
>
> *The Hows, Shoulds, and Coulda's*
> *All melt away*
> *When I stand in my power*
> *My heart leads the way*

The tough times I've faced
Were all part of the plan
My life is a lesson
A race that I ran

Now I'll teach you to dance
If you let yourself twirl
One step at a time
No weight of the world

    I am a tap and the water runs through me
    Saying goodbye to all those who knew me
    Fear is an anchor and love is a buoy

Choose your thoughts and your feelings
Weed your garden each day
Life is your instrument
Learn how to Play

Close your eyes, still your mind
I'll be with you, be certain
I'm here just beyond
This magical curtain

    I am a tap and the water runs through me
    Saying goodbye to all those who knew me
    Fear is an anchor and love is a buoy

UP

---

*"From a distance, you only see my light. Come
closer and know that I am you."*

—Rumi

et's talk about love. Not the garden variety between humans,
but the capital-L version. The kind of love that connects us
not just to ourselves and each other, but to something bigger.
Something magical. Yes, I believe in magic. Don't you? It's not often
a topic of conversation we open ourselves up to, perhaps because
it feels too intimate to give others a lens into our private relationship with the divine. "Divine *what?*" you ask? The simple answer
is, I don't know. But I do know that I believe in something-ness
rather than nothingness. That energy can't be extinguished, and
that you and I *are* energy. That *we* can't be extinguished. As Wayne
Dyer put it, "We are not human beings having a spiritual experience, we are spiritual beings having a human experience." I am
comfortable with the mystery. The not knowing.

"Sell your certainty and purchase bewilderment," said the great
Sufi poet, Rumi. To me, this quote speaks volumes about stepping
out of judgement and into curiosity. It also conjures our human

inclination to try to manage the world by labelling and sorting, placating ourselves with the illusion of control. I'm not here to make a case for spirituality, nor am I interested in convincing or converting you. In fact, I resist structure in this dimension. I've always found it so puzzling that the rules around religious belief are the cause of so much strife in our world.

God, Allah, Yahweh, Great Spirit, the Universe. Yes, yes, yes, yes, and yes. I accept it all. I also love the way many Indigenous cultures refer to this force as "Creator." After all, we are creators if nothing else. We create our lives, we create our relationships, we create art, and all too often, we create suffering. Thinking about the mystery as a greater creative force resonates for me. For the sake of this conversation, though, and to avoid any unintentional appropriation, I am suggesting a neutral name, one that fits with my theme in this book: Universal Presence—UP for short. Because yes, I do believe things are looking UP!

HOW FAITH FITS IN

"If we could but realize the sureness around us, we would be much more courageous in our lives. The frames of anxiety that keep us caged would dissolve. We would live the life we love and in that way, day by day, free our future from the weight of regret."
—John O'Donohue, *Beauty: The Invisible Embrace*

When I was mapping out this book, I kept resisting the subject of faith. Even though it's such an important part of my life, I was tempted to just skirt around it. I spent time contemplating why I'd been so reluctant to talk about my spirituality publicly. And one day I realized it was just another fear pothole, another facet of my life in which I was allowing potential judgements of others to dim my light.

One night during a wicked winter storm, I cozied up in front of the fire with a garden of candles on the table in front of me. Sitting there, relaxed and calm, I was suddenly struck by what I call a *bolt of enlightening*. I started to laugh out loud, finally seeing the humour in my indecision. How could I possibly write a book about Showing UP without being open about the role my spiritual beliefs play in my life? (Here's where I feel I should remind you about my initial message at the beginning of this book, of permission and possibility. If spirituality is not your jam, feel free to jump to the Doorways to Presence. You'll miss the magic, but you'll fast-forward to the more practical material.)

As you're reading this, you're welcome to picture me a bit like an addict standing at a first "meeting": "Hi, I'm Nancy, and I'm... spiritual." The author and teacher Caroline Myss says it perfectly in a YouTube video called *The Power of Prayer*: "I no longer...allow the absence of faith in other people to prevent me from talking about what the abundance of faith has brought me." She asks the audience if they know what she's saying, and there's a "Yes" in response. Then she continues, "The doubts that other people have no longer determine what I share with you." That is how I feel about including my take on spirituality in this book. If I'm going to completely remove my mask and Show UP with you, my reader, then my spirituality must necessarily be part of that revelation.

Is it a profound irony or a cosmic joke (or maybe both) that we spend our lives looking for love externally—when it has to be found first within? Even turning to divine love is often a pursuit outside ourselves, giving power to something bigger than us, but not owning our part of that divinity. Fear rules our lives when we feel disconnected, and freedom is found when we lean into love. That's when life gets easier.

FINDING THE DIVINE

"If you don't realize the source, you stumble in confusion and sorrow. When you realize where you come from, you naturally become tolerant, disinterested, amused, kindhearted as a grandmother, dignified as a king."
—Lao Tzu, *Tao Te Ching*

The King himself, Elvis Presley, could've probably used this ancient advice. He may not have been "dignified" when he was stumbling through his abusive relationship with drugs and alcohol, but he's another perplexing example of paradox. You may not know that I have a thing for Elvis. At the age of ten, I fell in love with his movies. When he died in 1977, I was shocked to see his changed appearance, and only then realized those films I'd been watching had been shot a decade or more before. Arguably the most ground-breaking performer of all time, and the most successful artist of his generation, Elvis also spent much of his life pursuing the mystery of spirituality.

In the book *The Seeker King: A Spiritual Biography of Elvis Presley* by Gary Tillery, Elvis is quoted as saying, "All I want is to know the truth, to know and experience God. I'm a searcher, that's what I'm all about." Included in the book is the story of Elvis and his entourage driving a deluxe motorhome through the Arizona desert on Route 66. In a moment of epiphany, Elvis hit the brakes and beckoned Larry Geller to follow him outside. Geller, Elvis's hairstylist, friend, and spiritual teacher, caught up to him and, standing there in the desert sand with tears on his face, Elvis said simply, "God is love, Larry. Now I know. I never have to doubt again."

My dear friend David Maginley is a rock star in his own realm, and his take on divinity aligns with this statement of Elvis's. David is an ordained minister, but his life's work is helping people with cancer navigate the psychological challenges of their disease. As an interfaith spiritual counsellor, he meets people wherever they are, and manages to connect with even the most resistant patients because of his down-to-earth approach. As he puts it, there's not a lot of starch in his collar. David's concept of God as love is the fulcrum of everything he does: "Love is not an emotion; it's the highest state of consciousness," he explains. "So, your spirituality will not be found in whatever your belief system is. It will be found in your love. So I'm going to focus on your love."

I asked David to sit down with me for a conversation while I was writing this chapter because I wanted to share his voice and his philosophy. I also felt I could never do the topic justice like he could. He was one of my first guests when I started *The Soul Booth* podcast, so I already knew his story well—including the astounding fact that he's survived cancer himself four times. Although he doesn't often volunteer this part of his story when working with patients, in his book, *Beyond Surviving*, David speaks openly about his near-death experience, when his heart stopped during his second round with cancer. It was a blissful encounter with a bright light that felt like pure love, and, as David says, a profound feeling of being "home." He believes he was sent back to Earth because he had important work do, and he's been living up to that edict ever since.

As we settled in for our chat, we got talking about how ego as the human identity keeps us grounded, but can also keep disconnected with what I'm calling Universal Presence. That's when David provided me with the best argument ever for committing to the present and keeping ego in check:

> We mistake the content for the clothing. We think it's permanent, and then the decades fly by and we discover none of it was. Why don't I remember my life? Well, because I didn't show up...in this moment. I was always looking at the other ones (that were just imagined). This moment is the only moment. Embed yourself in it. Don't expect anything grand or understandable, because it's not that small. Embed yourself in this moment. Be *apprehended* by this moment. You do not know who you are, and you cannot. Then emerge from this moment to be this amorphous, ambiguous, not-knowing, light...*being*.

I feel like I should pause here to let you read that again. Go ahead, I'll wait.

Okay, now take a deep breath, because we're just getting started. His next statement knocked my socks off: "Matter is just the densest form of spirit. The divine is everywhere, everything. God is."

On numerous occasions in my life, someone else's words have caused an instant shift in my understanding. This was one of them. *Matter is just the densest form of spirit.* Wow. I *felt* the truth of it. But my visual mind could also immediately accept it because of the obvious parallel to a substance we all need to survive—water! As we learned in high school chemistry, water can exist in three primary states: gas, liquid, and solid. Although we see it most often as fluid, it can also be steam, and of course, in its densest form, ice.

As soon as David said these words, I felt an extraordinary sense of understanding. Like he'd reminded me of something I'd always known to be true. And here's the funny thing. You know by now that I have a word fetish. I love dissecting language, seeing more than what's apparent in the whole word. Sometimes a whole world. Well, *dense* is a perfect description in this case.

When I was a kid in the 1970s, "You're so dense!" was the equivalent of "Duh" today, a word used to pejoratively suggest someone isn't all that bright. But when I heard David speak that day, it dawned on me that we, as humans, are exactly that. In the density of the matter we're made of, it can be hard to remember our connection to divine love. Particularly when we're disconnected from our own light. *When we're not that bright!* I was just regaining my equilibrium when David hit me with another Earth-shaking statement, this one thrown out casually with a mischievous grin: "I forget who said this, but we're all just angels who shit. We are this blend of the sacred and profane."

This line stopped me in my tracks because of our human proclivity to be so anchored in the physical, and focused on, well... shit! I thought immediately of Wayne Dyer, and how he might've loved this intersection of humour and profundity. Who knows; maybe Elvis would've, too. And this blatantly segues into what Wayne and Elvis had in common—apart from amazing stage presence. The two men, in different decades, and at different stages of their lives, became devoted to a book called *The Impersonal Life*.

The book was written in 1916 by a Lutheran minister by the name of Joseph Benner, who published it anonymously because he knew the work would compromise his position in the church. You see, Benner claims to have channelled the entire thing. It came *through* him, not from him, and while the spiritual concepts it related didn't mesh with the religious doctrine of his church, this clergyman knew the material had to be shared with the world. His name became associated with the book only after his death, when his wife revealed his authorship.

The book is written from the perspective of a higher being, but not from a higher place. It seeks to impress upon its reader that the voice is coming from *within*.

> But I AM *not* your human mind, nor its child, the intellect. They are but the expression of *your* Being, as you are the expression of *My* Being; they are but phases of your human personality, as You are a phase of My Divine Impersonality.

Here's the way I imagine this. Remember the Dimmer Theory, how you're born with a light within but it gets turned down through the struggles of life? And how, once you find your way through the tunnel of self-acceptance and actualization, you can turn your dimmer back up so that you are fully illuminated once again, and free to shine? When I visualize the concept of source within, I see it in terms of this light. For the sake of argument, consider a bonfire. If you and I are sitting in a group around a blazing fire, we can all reach a stick in and pull out our own flame. No matter how many of us do this the bonfire is not diminished, and yet we all have a piece of that original source of light and heat. We can grow it, or we can try to extinguish it—our choice. The book later describes how the self-consciousness of our body and intellect keep us "enslaved." For me, it's like we get trapped in our Earth mind; consumed with the mundane struggles of everyday life, we lose sight of our eternal nature. And there's a reason for that: we're programmed to forget.

I was fascinated to read Carl Jung's book *Memories, Dreams, Reflections* after reading *The Impersonal Life*, and to see how Joseph Benner's words align with Jung's description of himself. Jung describes realizing as a child that he seemed to have two "personalities." In fact, he called them "Number 1" and "Number 2." The first was his human identity, and the second was infinite—"having no definable character at all—born, living, dead, everything in one, a total vision of life." He came to refer to these two personalities as the ego and the self, and they are the basis of his theory of individuation. Many scholars point to this as evidence that Jung experienced a schizoid break or personality disorder. I'm no scholar, but the moment I learned of Jung's theory, it was abundantly clear to me that this representation aligned with his view of spirituality.

There are so many seemingly insurmountable challenges in our world today, so many reasons to be discouraged. We are under so much stress. What better medicine than the deepening of our spiritual practice, the embracing of our divinity? The more ways we can find to stay grounded while the world around us spins, the calmer and more effective we can be as parents, citizens, and leaders. But first, we have to tune into the frequency of the authentic self.

TUNING IN

I am the *hero* of my journey. And you are the hero of yours. But when we live out of alignment, in a vibration of static, we are the victims of our lives. Our lives are happening *to* us. It feels uncomfortable and out of control, so we often feel anxious, depressed, and unhappy. However, when we shift gears into a state of presence and passion, our lives begin unfolding *for* us. And this can only happen when we tune in.

I remember coming home from that retreat at Kripalu; I had walked the labyrinth and left behind baggage I hadn't even realized I was carrying. It was the first time in my life I experienced a prolonged period of joy. It was almost a sense of euphoria, and it persisted for two weeks. My husband and kids took notice, and no wonder. Before I left on my trip, I had been irritable and impatient; when I returned, I was calm, grateful, and emitting a loving frequency. I knew they liked this new version of me, but I also knew they were a little suspicious of just what was going on. I was a far cry from the burned-out perimenopausal wife and mother who had preceded me.

One day while walking the dogs in the park, I found myself wondering if this was a permanent shift. I knew it was a change for the better...but was it *for good*?! It wasn't. And as far as I can tell, it never is. Not unless you're an enlightened being, and for the record they are few and far between. I don't anticipate ever entering into that space of eternal calm. That's why it's a practice. From awakening, to sleeping, to awakening again. With compassion. But let me be clear on my metaphor here. You might expect that "sleeping" or "dreaming" would describe the euphoric state in which I can access self-love, but that would be a logical fallacy. When I'm *asleep*, I'm in the state of forgetting who and what I really am. *Awakening*, I'm remembering myself as light and love. And what a relief it is. Like floating in the sun on a calm ocean as opposed to fighting off a pack of hungry sharks.

The Tibetan master Tilopa once said, "Have a mind that is open to everything and attached to nothing." Wayne Dyer quoted this often, and it impacted my outlook deeply. So, here's an idea

I'd like you to consider rolling around in your head and heart, as you might savour a hard candy. What if you were part of a Soul Family, a group of eternal beings who love and support each other through physical lifetimes, each of which serve as a learning opportunity for spiritual growth? This is a thought framework that has helped me overcome much resentment in my life, and to embrace forgiveness. After all, the hardest things I've gone through have triggered the most personal growth, so I can honestly say that the people who've challenged me most are the ones who have enabled my expansion. And to be clear, "expansion" sounds lovely, but in my experience, it usually hurts like hell.

One thing that hurts a little less with this perspective, is grief. I wrote this on the last weekend we shared with Audrey at the cottage, less than a month before her death.

When I woke this morning, there was an enormous fog bank hanging heavy over the beach below. It was dense and dark. Yet above the distinct upper edge was sunshine and blue sky. I immediately felt grateful for this perfect visual representation of how I'm feeling right now.

Before I can round up the dogs and head for the water, the scene has shifted noticeably—sun now melting the troubled sky like watercolours dripping down a canvas. Leashes taut, I am pulled toward the energy of the ocean, and the beauty that is created by the meeting of the waves and land.

High tide forces me to walk the rocks, so I'm necessarily in the moment, finding my footing step by step. Much like this journey toward November 1st. Everywhere I look, and every thought I think this morning, wraps me in metaphor. When I fold my arms across my chest for warmth, I correct myself, seeing the symbolism. It's so tempting to try to shut out the emotion, to try to shield my heart. Instead, I unfold my arms and open up to the chill, but also to the sun. Audrey hasn't folded inward. She's done the opposite, like the professional dancer she used to be, head up, shoulders back, chest open. Heart open.

The synchronicity of a heart-shaped stone makes me smile. Love is swirling around us all right now. The support and care we're giving Aud is simply a reverberation of what she gives us every day. By showing us how to die, she's teaching us how to live. But she's not just teaching her friends. People she's never met are reaching out with words full of meaning, full of gratitude and grief. Gratitude and grief—seemingly foes, but actually brothers. One can't be without the other.

I feel enormous gratitude to have had this woman in my life, to have walked this path with her. But the grief I'm facing at my impending loss is a shadow in the morning sun...equal in size and omnipresent. Just a few weeks from her scheduled death, Aud says she feels she's already starting her spiritual transition, and my sorrow is growing every day as if it's already happening.

But wait...30 minutes ago the fog obscured the view, and now I'm looking at a brilliant blue sky. This dramatic difference will remain etched in my mind. She won't be gone, only out of sight. Out of touch, but not out of mind or heart.

My breathing fills out in my chest, and my body unclenches as I stand back and see the whole picture. My eyes go back to the stones underfoot. There's a remarkable variety of shapes, colours, and patterns, like the plethora of friends Audrey has accumulated in her life. Her rare breed of authenticity has lent her a powerful magnetism, which has been amplified in this final chapter. Sitting in her "Bed of Truth," she welcomes in everyone like the Empress she is.

The waves dance beside me. Their ebb and flow reminds me of how fleeting time is. It's mesmerizing to watch the breeze icing the wave-tops with mist. It hangs in mid-air, sparkling in the sunlight for a moment, and then it's gone, bringing me into the now. I think of Dave Carroll's beautiful song "Now," and how Audrey has given deep meaning to its first line. "When there's no way out, there's still a way through."

Dave wrote that song because he was inspired by Eckhart Tolle's book *The Power of Now*, a book about the transformative power of presence. Audrey's present is a gift to us all. And her presence won't be extinguished by her death, only expanded. It'll be up to those of us left standing on the beach to remember—she's just beyond the fog.

> death is just a fog bank
> on the beaches of our hearts
> we lose sight of our horizons
> as we grieve and fall apart
>
> but the sun's still there
> beyond the mist
> and when the spirits lift
> our face is warmed once more by love
> and we learn life's greatest gift
>
> we're souls before we're physical
> each day alive's a dream

we're not a wave upon the sand
we're an everlasting Stream

Audrey was strangely excited about finding out what came *next*, and because she was in the unique position of knowing exactly when and how she was going to die, she often mused about what was awaiting her on the other side. "Maybe it'll just be the end, and there'll be nothing," she would say, seeking to be pragmatic, "but I really don't think so. I can't wait to see what happens!"

———————

They say faith is believing in something even without evidence, but I see evidence all the time. Signs that there is something greater at play in our lives than the mundanity of the everyday. My aforementioned friend Anne Bérubé recently published her second book, *The Burnout Antidote*, and I'm happy to say that I had the pleasure of watching it come to life. For a few years now, Anne and I have been in the delightful practice of escaping together for cottage writing retreats. Just the two of us, revelling in the natural setting and the opportunity to step out of our busy lives and focus on our books. Our habit is to write silently through the day, and then talk over supper and into the evening. It's transformative, and there always seems to be magic swirling around us, but there was one twenty-four-hour period I'll never forget.

In February 2021, with COVID-19 temporarily on the back burner in Nova Scotia, Anne and I embarked on one such getaway. One evening, just as the light was fading and the sun was drifting toward the horizon, I happened to mention that I was going to have a Zoom call later that night with my husband's family. It was the second anniversary of my brother-in-law's passing. He had died suddenly of a heart attack at fifty-eight, while shovelling snow. It was a horrific shock to the whole family, like a heart attack to our collective system, because he'd been so full of life. His heart might have been technically faulty, or it might have just worn out from the lifetime of love he heaped on all those around him. As I told Anne, he was probably the most positive and enthusiastic person I'd ever met, and it was impossible to imagine a life force like his extinguished.

Within thirty seconds of that comment, I was passing by a window when something in the field right below the house caught my eye: a beautiful procession of ten deer. I knew that, from her perch, Anne couldn't see them yet, but they would soon appear right in front of the window she was facing. I smiled mischievously and said, "Oh, you're in for quite a treat...!" Then I went over and stood beside her chair, and within moments they were all framed like a painting in that pane of glass.

We were marvelling at the serene beauty of these animals when the largest of the pack started prancing around, very obviously trying to engage the others in play. Then, like a bolt, he took off, running at full speed in the direction from which they had come. Once he got to the end of the field, he made a sharp turn and ran, full-tilt, all the way back. Once again, he pranced among his pack, as if in the hope that his fun energy would be contagious. Anne and I were shocked, until I broke our open-mouthed silence with a simple, "There he is." Anne knew exactly what I meant. It was Billy energy. I had just spoken of his unparalleled zest for life, and that's how he showed up. Awed by this divinely timed visit, Anne and I laughed in delight. And never one to let a corny pun pass me by, I joined in the fun, yelling out toward the field, "I love you, Deer!"

Just a few hours later, the subject came up again when we were sitting by a dying fire. We had stopped feeding it fresh logs because we were almost ready for bed, the remnants of wood in the grate now just glowing embers. Anne and I were winding down too, feeling grateful for a rich writing day and still marvelling at the way spirit showed up in synchronicity; how that connection is so available to us when we are firmly (and gently) planted in the present. It's like tapping into an electrical current, and each time you have this experience it opens you up a little more to the next time. But Anne and I were in different places on this path. Like the title of Wayne Dyer's book, *You'll See it When You Believe It*, Anne was already a believer. Skeptical by nature, I was becoming one only as I saw proof. This difference in openness had a lot to do with how much time I've spent Showing Off and not Showing UP.

The first time I heard Anne talking to an audience about having had visits from Wayne Dyer after his death, I cringed, worried about what people would think. Please know, it wasn't that I didn't believe her. I'd witnessed how close Anne had been to Wayne and I loved hearing about how he sent her messages "from beyond." I'd even been present for some of these mystical moments (which is not a surprise, given that Anne and I were brought together by Wayne's tour, and spent time with him just months before his passing), but talking about it in public? No way. However, I did find that when I was with like-minded friends in private, removed from the fear of others' judgement, I was able to Show UP fully.

That evening by the fire, I started telling Anne about how Audrey had coached those closest to her to watch for signs from her. She had actually been excited about that aspect of her end-of-life experience. At one point she'd decided that coins were going to be her thing; that whenever we happened upon a nickel, it was her sending us a sign. But as I told Anne that night, my response had been quick: "Aud, you're underestimating your power. You're going to be able to rock all the signs!" Audrey had chuckled and agreed I was probably right.

I had no idea how right I'd turn out to be.

I was describing to Anne how connected I feel when I take time to find stillness in my life, how much I feel Audrey's presence, and how many different signs she does send, when suddenly the barely glowing embers in the fireplace burst into flame. It was as if we'd tossed in gasoline. Anne and I stared for a moment at the fire, and then at each other, and burst into astonished laughter. Anne said, "There you go—if that's not confirmation, I don't know what is!" As we watched, the flame continued to grow—even though we hadn't fed it any wood for over an hour. I went to bed that night feeling a deeper sense of spiritual connection than I had ever known before. I guess I had to see it to believe it!

We left the next morning, feeling gratified and grateful on the heels of a productive and fulfilling week. But as we were packing the car, something happened to finish off our stay in style. A commotion above us attracted our attention, and we looked up to see a magnificent bald eagle landing on the top of a pine tree. As it gazed down at us, looking peaceful and proud, Anne and I were frozen in the moment. Then, we were simultaneously struck with a realization that caused immediate laughter. The bird's big white bald head had conjured an image of Wayne Dyer. I turned to Anne and repeated a line we've said many times to one another: "You really can't make this shit up!"

As I write this, I'm shocked by my own willingness to reveal my mystical side. But now that I've thrown the door open, I might as well fly right through! These stories are my way of sharing the gifts of love and peace I feel when I'm truly present. If you're feeling unsure about it all, that's okay. If I had read something like this a decade ago, I might've found it intriguing and uncomfortable at the same time. But that was before I came to see myself as an instrument. And that's where truth bumps come in. You probably call them "goose bumps," but I'm talking about that physical feeling that happens when you experience a weird sense of "knowing," or an unexplainable "coincidence." Sometimes it comes with a chill or makes the hair on the back of your neck stand up, but however you describe it, it happens to me a lot. The more spiritually centred I become, the more I notice it. I call them truth bumps because I believe they're caused by spirit dancing around me, saying, "Yeah, baby...you're getting it!"

––––––––––––

Another meteoric example I'll share occurred after my friend Ken died at home after an eight-month odyssey with glioblastoma. Here's my journal entry from that night:

> I lost a beautiful friend tonight, and the world lost a beautiful human. But although he has departed this physical plane, Ken apparently hasn't gone far. His spirit has left his body by the time I arrive in the room, and I join Karen and Aria (his wife and twenty-year-old daughter) at his bedside.
>
> Have you ever considered the word used to describe the dead, "the remains"? I think of it as just that: what's left behind when the soul leaves. As with the other times I've seen the dead bodies of people I love, it actually gives me comfort to be in the presence of this vessel that so clearly is not Ken. Karen and Aria and I sit with him and toast his life with a glass of champagne,

allowing tears to flow, but also smiling and laughing as we reminisce about his amazing journey.

Eventually the men from the funeral home come, and I volunteer to sit on the back deck with Donner (a 120-pound Bernese mountain dog) to keep him from barking. It's a chilly October night, and for the first few minutes I sit in a chair, leaning down to pat this huge dog who had loved Ken so fiercely. But then, I decide to slip down onto the deck and sit beside Donner. The moment my perspective shifts, I can see the night sky. And within three seconds, the most breathtaking thing happens. A huge fireball suddenly streaks across the sky, startling me. There are fiery pieces breaking off, and it seems so big and so close that I think for a moment it's an aircraft in flames. But then it disappears into nothingness. Or into everything-ness.

When Karen and Aria open the sliding door a couple minutes later, I'm still vibrating. I tell them about what I just saw and instantly, Aria's sweet young face is transfigured as she starts to sob. "That's what I asked for!" she exclaims, pushing her way through the door and out onto the deck. Halfway between tears and laughter, she talks a mile a minute about how she and her dad always loved looking at the starry sky together—talking about the Milky Way, shooting stars, meteors, and black holes. As it turned out, just a couple of weeks ago at the cottage, Aria had asked Ken to give her a sign in the starry sky when he passed. I sit there silenced by the shock of it all, and also in fear that she will resent me for seeing her sign.

Then I hear the words come out of my mouth calmly like someone else is saying them: "I was the one outside, and I was meant to see that meteor to give you the message right

*at the moment you needed it most." They were just about
to carry Ken's body out the door, and that meteor reminded
us all that it was just the physical matter that "remained" of
him on the stretcher.*

So yes, I believe that when we are open to receiving messages from other dimensions, we can. I wouldn't call myself a psychic, but I do think we all have psychic abilities; that we're *all* equipped for communication—like radios. Consider this: radios just broadcast static if they're not tuned in to a channel. And for us humans, presence is a prerequisite for tuning. Many experiences have led me to this conclusion, and now I'm comfortable sharing.

Well, I'm getting there.

––––––––––––

Many artists, musicians, and writers rely on their connection to Universal Presence (UP) for their creative motivation. Whenever I hear the word "inspiration," I think of the Latin *in spiritu,* or "in spirit." I feel this most when I write poetry. My grandmother Rose was a poet, and although she died before I was born, I feel a strong connection to her. When a poem drops into my head like a parachutist landing, I know Rose is ready to collaborate.

> *My grandmothers rise
> in me
> They do not sit
> knitting quietly in rocking chairs
> They stand
> in full expressions
> of themselves*

They inspire me
In Spiritu

They breathe
life into my lungs
love into my heart
ideas into my mind

no longer tied down
by their generations' generalizations
they are free
they are fierce
they are fire

and so—
am I

CONTROL VERSUS SURRENDER

A Course in Miracles is a book that was published in the 1970s. Billed as a self-study course for spiritual development, it has been the basis for many such books since. The primary idea contained within is that everything—every emotion, every thought, every action—can be boiled down to a fundamental motivation: fear or love. *I want them to like me* = fear. *I'm here to help* = love. It's really quite a simple concept; you don't have to do the year-long course to incorporate this philosophy into your life and experience its transformative power. I haven't ever done the course, but I've read sections, and loved Marianne Williamson's summary of its principles in her book *A Return to Love*.

In presence, I can catch myself in a moment of distrust, resentment, or doubt and recognize the fear lurking behind it. And then the challenge is to see my fear and myself with compassion. Scarcity is a fertile example. This fear-based mindset seems to be my default setting: a constant concern that there won't be enough (money, time, attention). A mindset of abundance, on the other hand, is an outgrowth of love. As I embraced this way of looking at life, I came to understand how profoundly fear has held me back. Fear forces me into *surviving* rather than *thriving*, reluctance rather than enthusiasm, negating rather than nurturing, caution rather than adventure, stress rather than joy, absence rather than presence. It makes me the victim of my life instead of the hero.

When we let go of what's been weighing us down, we discover a way forward that is bright, rewarding, and joyful. One of those weights for me was my Gator, GUS. When I resisted him, he reacted like a demanding child being ignored, getting louder and more persistent. So I finally asked myself, is fear my enemy? No. he's my ally. Talk about comic relief...as it turns out, GUS is my ALLY-GATOR! And on that note, I think it's time I finally share with you my letter from fear.

Dear Nancy, Why do you insist on treating me like shit? I am the only one who's never left you. Never let you down. I have witnessed many people hurt you, but still you wrestle with my instincts like I am the enemy. I am on your side. Why can't you see that? No matter how adept you are at convincing other humans that you're strong, I know how weak you are. I know you're hungry for a love that will fortify you. Prop you up and make you whole. It doesn't exist outside of you, so my job is to protect you from disappointment. I am loyal, fierce, and

hard-working. Please see me. Let me be. Protecting you from
loss, embarrassment, humiliation, injury, and failure is a big
job. 24-7. Lousy pay, no perks, no pension...but here I still am.
I am stronger than you and I know all the ways in which your
life can go off the rails. Be afraid. Please! I love you, GUS

There is a line in Liz Gilbert's book *Big Magic* that sums up my
relationship with fear beautifully: "It seems to me that the less
I fight my fear, the less it fights back. If I can relax, fear relaxes
too." I used to think I had to overcome fear, that I had to eradicate
my gator. But like so many things in my life, resistance doesn't
solve the problem. I had to learn to befriend my fear. I had to let
my gator *be*. However, that doesn't mean I allow him to run my
life. He still tends to sneak up on me, so I've had a soulful security system installed. A little imaginary bell rings in my head the
moment I sense the gator growing. You see, learning to love GUS
was like a scene out of the movie *Honey, I Shrunk the Kids*. As I
began to regard my fear with compassion and understanding, he
was transformed.

It happened in North Caicos. I was sitting alone in a tiki
hut when suddenly, a colourful little creature interrupted my
pre-writing meditation by scrambling across my foot. I jumped
a little, but I didn't scream as I normally would have. This gecko
seemed too obviously meant to be there with me. He had been
hanging around all week, appearing at auspicious moments. And
this moment felt auspicious. When I'd initially sat down to write,
I'd taken a deep breath, allowing the salt air to fill my lungs, while
I gazed gratefully at the turquoise water just a few feet away. I
reached for a book about synchronicity lying on the table next to
me and opened it to a random page, looking for a message. The
page I landed on was all about creativity—just as I was sitting

down to write. How perfect is that? Then I happily closed my eyes to allow my body and brain to calm. That's when my friend the gecko happened onto my foot, his arrival a clear sign of a muse.

In my mind, he was there to inspire me, so I immediately contemplated how he might represent an unleashing of my creative juices. Apart from his intricately designed back, he had a long and flexible tail. As he sat attentively surveying his surroundings, he looked very much like he was in upward dog or cobra pose. It struck me that he was utterly and completely in the moment—he wasn't worried about what was going to happen that afternoon or what happened yesterday. His scaly skin represented layers that would peel off when he was done with them, revealing a new version, a new self. He had such a wild sense of freedom. Able and eager to crawl on any surface, horizontal or vertical. Entirely comfortable with the gaze of beings around him. Not performing but also not being inhibited by their presence, their judgement, or their sense of comfort—or lack thereof.

I broke into a smile as I realized that—at that moment—I was like a gecko. Alert, yet calm. Adventurous, yet grounded. Loving, yet committed to not abandoning myself. Even just observing this small, earthbound creature anchored me in the moment. Nowhere but here. *Be here now.* That's what my gecko friend taught me. I accepted his gift of energy and set an intention to lock it into the light that comes with the transformation from fear to love. Who would'a thunk I could love a lizard!? I nearly shrieked when the deeper meaning of his visit occurred to me. With the right kind of attention and affection, I could shrink GUS, my gator, into a gecko.

And now I ask you to reflect on this: How can you reduce *your* reptile, and engage your curiosity to convert fear to love? Maybe the first step is not to think of them as opposites, but as co-existing, part of a spectrum on which we seek balance.

FROM FEAR TO SPHERE

Richard Rohr is a Franciscan friar and a globally popular thought leader. The first time I saw him speak, he *broke open* my perspective on life with his take on non-duality. He was describing contemplation as an old form of prayer that Christianity has lost sight of. Instead of asking for favours or protection, contemplation is all about sitting with what *is*. It is about acceptance. Our world is drowning in duality. Good or bad, right or wrong, gay or straight, black or white. We live in division. But imagine a different vision, one not ruled by ego and fear, but powered by love. Where we're connected, to ourselves and to each other, and to something bigger than us. Perfection takes on a whole new meaning in a frame of non-duality. There's no room for perfectionism because *perfect* is a condition beyond our control. Perfection is *what is*.

> *It isn't supposed to be like this*
> *said the woman on the beach*
> *She'd been counting hard on sunshine*
> *to bring happiness*
> *within reach*
> *If only for an hour, or a wave upon the sand*
> *she'd wed her spirits to the weather*
> *and failed to*
> *understand*
> *The fog is just an impediment*
> *if we allow it to be so*
> *The wind is not a villain*

no matter how
it blows

Our nemesis lies within the mind
in a dark and sticky lair
It rules our lives and darkens our days
till we become aware
Awakening to reality
accepting whatever is
brings us into the moment
and connects us to our bliss

Paul Luftenegger's newest album of what he calls "conscious music" is called *Spheres of Love*, and that title is very intentional. It stems from Paul's visual theory of human beings as full circles encompassing everything...orbs of divine love, with no end and no beginning. No duality. Everything accepted in the sphere and nothing left out. When I first heard his explanation, I immediately saw myself as a wineglass. Not quite a sphere, but close. It was a reflection of my own awareness that I can feel full of my own light, full of love, but I can also get knocked over and have it all spill out. Is this negativity or self-awareness? Yes and yes. (By the way, one of the songs on *Spheres of Love*, "Broken and Whole," was partially inspired by my *Soul Booth* conversation with Liz Gilbert, and it's a gorgeous tribute to paradox.)

The more I am willing to be vulnerable, to reveal my own struggles with inadequacy, the more it becomes clear that this quest is a natural part of the human experience. I've been floored by the number of people who can relate. It's the reason behind this book. I believe that's because in being human, we're programmed to forget our own divinity. Our *density*. As William Wordsworth put it, "Our birth is but a sleep and a forgetting." Forgetting, I fall into the false belief that things outside myself can make me happy. Awakening, I remember I need nothing to be whole. Seeing myself as a sphere has brought me to a surprising conclusion; that I am my own soulmate.

Allow me to explain. There's an iconic scene in the film *Jerry Maguire*, where Tom Cruise's character, Jerry, declares his love for Renée Zellweger's character, Dorothy. "You complete me" is the enduring quote from that speech, but it highlights our human need for external validation and fulfillment. It seems to me, the concept of soulmates has rendered a generation of women unhappy and unsatisfied. We watch romantic movies and buy into the notion that there's one person out there who's going to come along and make us whole. The truth is—and it has taken me a lifetime to realize this—I don't need someone else to complete me. I don't need a spotlight shining on me to light me up, and I don't need approval to be *enough*. My value is not established by the opinions of others, and I don't *need* to be seen as enough by anyone but myself. Self-love and self-compassion are what completes the sphere.

And then of course, the next step is to apply this concept to others. To see human frailty and respond with love. Like paradox, non-duality allows love and fear to coexist. Because of the safety of the sphere, fear's role is appropriately minimized. I dream of a world where we can all dance together in love instead of running in fear. Where we can move from fear to sphere. Spheres hold paradox in comfort. If we can see each other as spheres that contain the wonder and the wounds, we can step out of the habit of "othering" and embrace our connectedness. My many interviews with celebrities have left me with an enduring understanding that we are *all the same*. We laugh, we lose, and we love. We also hurt and hide, and we have the power to help. In fact, I believe we're *here* to help.

In our personal practice, this movement away from duality and toward acceptance means exploring the difference between prayer and contemplation. One prayer in particular, "Our Father," was a constant part of my childhood and you are likely familiar with it. Between saying it aloud at bedtime, and then again in Sunday mass, I repeated it thousands of times during my youth. It was even recited at the beginning of each day in elementary school. I know it by heart, but it no longer resonates in my soul. One day I made a creative practice out of rewording it, just for myself, to better reflect my evolving spiritual beliefs. I don't mean to offend anyone who is attached to the original. I am not prescribing what you or anyone else should *believe*. But here's what I came up with for myself:

> Universal Presence that unites us all in love, I am grateful for your light in my life. Help me to remember my connection to your divine love, allowing me to feel it profoundly and share it generously. May I be grounded by this knowing so as to be of joyful service.

This felt good—even right—for a while, but I soon I became uncomfortable with its extrinsic nature, as if I were pleading for favour to be shone on me by a parental figure. It felt a bit like ego was leading the way, like I was relying on being "special." Then one day, a new prayer awakened in me.

The day before, my daughter had been going through an old stash of bath bombs and commented on how cool it was that smells could evoke vivid memories. I agreed, and told her there's even a name for this seemingly magical phenomenon: a "Proustian moment," named after Marcel Proust, who was the first to coin the term "involuntary memory." I gave her a quick and dirty to others. You may recognize this imagery from earlier. My new personal prayer is rooted in the rich soil of Edith Wharton's quote, "There are two ways of spreading light; to be the candle or the mirror that reflects it," and the work of Richard Rohr, whose explanation of one small word was philosophically explosive for me.

But first, let me take you back a minute. If you're old enough, you may remember the Saturday morning *Schoolhouse Rock* animated shorts. (Even if you're not, I'm happy to say they live on, on YouTube.) The series explained educational topics for children through catchy music and entertaining visuals. The episode I'm thinking of right now is *Conjunction Junction*—a 1973 animation that celebrates the merits of words like *and*, *but*, and *or*. The power of conjunctions is visually represented by a busy train yard where these words are essential for joining words and phrases (boxcars) to create sentences (trains). You may be wondering where I'm going with this, but here's how it connects to my contemplative prayer. Richard Rohr is not only a revered teacher and thought leader, he's also the founder of an organization called the Center for Action and Contemplation—a title that holds a world of meaning. He describes "and" as the most potent word in the centre's name because it's about *integrating* contemplation and action.

I'm going to invite you into a different visual image now. Picture a pendulum with these two words—"Contemplation" and "Action"—at opposing ends. It's in the middle—in the "and"— where the best stuff happens. In much the same way a conjunction is devoid of meaning unless anchored by the words around it (the conjuncts), action that is not anchored by contemplation can be futile. And so can contemplation be without action. However, the marriage of contemplative prayer and *purpose* propels us into joyful service. So here's the point. To me, spirituality is not about sitting on a mat and being blissed out. It's about finding a way to bring that bliss into your everyday life, and using it as fuel for changing the world for the better. Putting your train on the track and making it mean something.

CONTRIBUTION

*"The problem with the world is that we draw
the circle of our family too small."*
—Mother Teresa

I was listening to a podcast one day when I first heard Father Richard Rohr's voice, and it was these words of his that stopped me in my tracks: "...where knowing is balanced by unknowing, which by the way is the core meaning of faith." Rohr has written that faith and doubt are not opposites but "correlatives," meaning they have a mutual relationship. In this instance, doubt plays an important role in deepening faith. Rohr cites the example of Mother Teresa, who experienced decades of struggle in her relationship with God and scandalized the world by revealing her doubt. But if we frame this in another way, her doubt was just an element of contemplation, of sitting with what *is* and being in the mystery. According to a *Time* magazine article on the subject, while "Teresa considered the perceived absence of God in her life as her most shameful secret...she eventually learned that it could be seen as a gift abetting her calling." Mother Teresa accepted that doubt was part of her experience of faith, just as we must accept that fear is part of love. And it is all part of our human experience.

On its website, the Center for Action and Contemplation describes its philosophy:

Amidst a time of planetary change and disruption, we envision a recovery of our deep connection to each other and our world, led by Christian and other spiritual movements that are freeing leaders and communities to overcome dehumanizing systems of oppression and cooperate in the transforming work of Love.

The "transforming work of Love." That phrase echoes in my soul. It's also a reminder that there is work to be done. Spirituality isn't just about sitting in meditation and sending good vibes out into the Universe. It's about contributing to the world around you.

It's my belief that contribution is not energetically clear when we are Showing Off. In my experience, in order to make a meaningful impact, I needed to get out of my own way. Over and over again. I needed to stop worrying about my attachment to my mask, to stop looking for approval and fearing judgement. I learned this in a vivid way through the writing of this book, and at some point it dawned on me that this lesson is the exact same tenet that I drive home with my presentation clients: if you're on stage thinking about your performance, you're not serving your audience or yourself. It's not until you shift your focus to the *contribution* you're there to make that your light will truly shine! In other words: it's about giving, not getting.

This is true in terms of pursuing your life's purpose as well. If your intention is to be of service and you connect that to your inner light, you will help illuminate the darkness for those you help. Oprah did this for me, and for millions. I have so much respect for how she chose to break boundaries in the 1980s when she began a soulful exchange with her TV audience. I remember when she spoke to Gary Zukav about his book *The Seat of the Soul*.

This was groundbreaking in the world of network television, but Oprah tapped into an unspoken longing for something *more* in our lives. She took a chance, put her reputation on the line, and the gamble paid off. That turned out to be the first of thirty-five conversations they'd share over the years, and Zukav's wisdom appears to have served up a lot of "Aha moments" for the Queen of Talk. In fact, their ongoing dialogue probably laid the groundwork for her *Super Soul Sunday* series, which is still going strong more than a decade after first airing. Oprah is one of the most powerful people on the planet, and her definition of power seems to be derived from this passage from Zukav's book:

> When we align our thoughts, emotions, and actions with the highest part of ourselves, we are filled with enthusiasm, purpose, and meaning....When the personality comes fully to serve the energy of its soul, that is authentic empowerment.

Oprah demonstrated how she has internalized this philosophy of Zukav's in a column titled "What Oprah Knows for Sure About Real Power":

> For me, there is no real power without spiritual power. (A power that comes from the core of who you are and reflects all that you were meant to be.) A power that's connected to the source of things. When you see this kind of power shining through someone in all its truth and certainty, it's irresistible, inspiring, elevating.

It's just that kind of power that shines through Oprah, and it explains her global popularity. Another much-loved example is

The Dalai Lama. He is quoted in *The Book of Joy* as saying "Too much self-centred thinking is the source of suffering. A compassionate concern for others' wellbeing is the source of happiness." While I agree with the latter statement, I also believe we *need* to turn within to remember our light. Only through learning to see ourselves with love and compassion can we intensify that light, and then feel comfortable sharing it. And there is a paradigm shift when we move our focus from "What will the neighbours think?" to "How can I be of service in my neighbourhood?"—whether that is your community, your country, or the world.

"Joyful service" is a phrase I first heard from David Maginley, and these two words have become my guiding force. I have many friends who follow this principle, and their simple morning prayers range from "How may I be of service?" to "Love through me." The second one belongs to David, and that's exactly how he shows up in the world—as an instrument of love, supporting strangers through the most challenging time of their lives.

Honing *instruments* like this is the craft of the Halifax-based socially minded coaching program Soulo Projects, which is focused on helping soul-driven individuals find and embrace their purpose and passion. I participated in the program a few years ago, and it not only created the spark that led to this book project—it gave me the motivation and mechanism to make it happen. There are a lot of people like me who love what we do so much, we'd be content to do it for free, but the Soulo Projects manifesto sums up the philosophy that shapes us into entrepreneurs:

I believe: in being of service, in building community, in making a difference in the lives of others, in the power of personal stories, and that purpose is the most solid foundation on which to build a business.

Having sufficient money for the staples of life (food, housing, etc) is necessary for a sense of personal security, but a lot of people spend their lives longing to be rich, expecting that wealth is going to somehow bring happiness and peace. I believe what they're really craving, without knowing it, is to be *en*riched. I revel in meeting those who've travelled the path from a material mindset to the expansive realization that what is truly enriching is living a purpose-driven life. I don't want to pretend that purpose is straightforward. When I was wandering in the metaphorical wilderness, it was tremendously frustrating to hear people talk about how *rich* life becomes when you find your true purpose. I was desperate to figure out what my own purpose was, but having no success. The thing is, I was searching in the dark when what I needed to find was the light. I was running in circles chasing my tail when I really just needed to sit still.

That's how the practice of presence changed everything. It helped transform my relationship with myself, with others, with the world around me, and it allowed me to lean in to the mystery. It led me to the sense of purpose I feel deeply now. Whether I'm interviewing someone for a podcast or coaching a client to feel more at ease on stage, it's all about stoking *their* fire. My light is brightened by helping other people learn to shine—onstage and off. There's nothing more gratifying than watching someone discover, celebrate, and share their own luminous self.

I'm not a life coach. I'm a light coach.

And the light in me honours, and celebrates, the light in you.

TAPPING INTO PRESENCE

Before we discover some of the Doorways to Presence, I want to leave you with this journal entry, as a way of transitioning from thought to action, from theory to experience.

It sits in the grass, idle; not an interesting source of anything. Full of holes and full of potential but not of service. And it has no idea that service is its purpose. But then, the tap gets turned on, and the water starts to flow. It may be interrupted at first because of a kink in the hose, or perhaps a faulty connection, but when the obstacles are eliminated the fun begins!

The sprinkler explodes into action, water streaming through the air, providing nourishment for the grass and soil. Children nearby react with wonder, amazement, and delight. Some are drawn to it immediately, eager to get wet—yet often tentative about immersing themselves in this new flow. Some flirt with the water—first their feet, then their legs, then their glee propels their whole bodies into the arc, allowing the water to soak them. Others stand back, watching in interest, but reluctant to get wet. Afraid of the cold jets. Safe on the sidelines, but intrigued. Still others walk away, not seeing the glory, or not interested in this invitation to play.

To let go, to be joy. This is presence—not everyone is comfortable stepping into it. It is allowing. It is NOW.

I want to be that sprinkler. Usefulness animates me. When I collaborate with Universal Presence in creativity, I feel the rush of energy through me like water from the tap. Keeping it to myself is not an option.

Expensive sprinklers come with a switch to control their output, so the tap can be turned on fully but the flow is stilled. Some water may leak from the holes or the connection, but the promise and beauty are captive when unleashed. This state is more dynamic than before the tap was turned on, but there's a stagnancy even in its energetic fullness. *Stag-Nancy.* That's what I'm leaving behind. I'm opening my gauge to High. Hi! What flows through me is not *from* me. I do not seek nor deserve approval for it. I am planted in Rumi's field—beyond ideas of wrong-doing and right-doing. I will meet you *here. Now.*

I promise, I'll Show UP.

Will you?

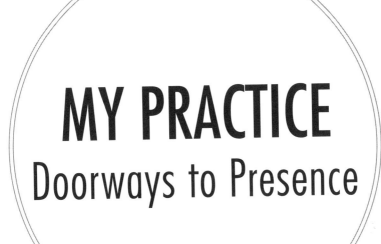

MY PRACTICE
Doorways to Presence

COME TO YOUR SENSES

"For most of us, there is only the unattended
Moment, the moment in and out of time...
the waterfall, or music heard so deeply
That it is not heard at all, but you are the music
While the music lasts."

—T. S. Eliot, Four Quartets, "The Dry Salvages," 1941

For a long time, I thought I had to *learn* to love myself; that I had to labour away to silence the voice of my inner critic. I was right—to a point. It took a dedication to the cause: books as stepping stones, teachers as guides, a commitment to the labyrinth that is the path. I marched on like a soldier desperate to win the war. But here's the thing: I didn't need to *learn*, I just had to remember. I simply had to remove the obstacles to self-love: obstacles from the past and the future. The reward for remembering is peace. I have retired my weapons. Stepped out of my combat boots in favour of bare feet in the sand and sun on my face. And you can too.

The following is my pay-it-forward, a garden of ideas fertilized with gratitude and tended with love. Pick whichever flowers bloom for you and leave the rest to compost. You never know... shit that doesn't help you now might come in handy in the future!

Use these pages to help you settle into the present and remember: you are strong, beautiful, and worthy of love. You are perfect. Imperfectly perfect.

Okay, I have a question for you. *Where are you now?* I mean right now. Stop reading for a moment, take a deep breath, and just be *here*. Every once in a while, I'm going to ask you this question that I ask myself multiple times each day. It does two things for me: it brings me fully into the present moment, and it makes me laugh.

The humour is found in the question's origin story. It's a reminder of Wayne Dyer, who, as I've explained, had quite an impact on my spiritual growth. One day, shortly after he died, I was walking on the beach thinking about him and I silently asked the question, "Where are you now, Wayne?" Immediately, I heard the question echo back to me: "Where are *you* now?" I chuckled and thought, *touché!* But then it dawned on me: these words offered a tool I could use to bring me back to the present. After weeks of using this little trick successfully, I decided to create an acronym. You should've seen my jaw drop when I realized the initials spelled out WAYN. The next moment, I knew he had also answered my question: "Where are you now?"...*Everywhere.* W.A.Y.N.E.

I remember years ago hearing Eckhart Tolle, whose work has taught me so much about being present, suggest a similar question during an interview. He said simply, "Ask yourself, 'am I breathing?'" As he describes it, breath forces you into the present moment. This was extremely helpful in my life. My monkey mind spends all day every day swinging wildly from past to future if I let it. I'm either ruminating about something that's already happened or worrying about something that might. And in that swirl, I'm often not breathing well. More on the breath later—but now let's talk about *now*!

It was earth-shaking when I first learned, in Tolle's book *The Power of Now*, that psychological negativity is typically found somewhere other than the present. "Unease, anxiety, tension, stress, worry—all forms of fear—are caused by too much future, and not enough presence," he wrote. "Guilt, regret, resentment, grievances, sadness, bitterness, and all forms of non-forgiveness are caused by too much past, and not enough presence."

That paragraph stopped me in my tracks, and when I took some time to think about it through the filter of my life, it blew my mind. Blew it right into the here and now.

Be Here Now is the title of a 1971 book by the late spiritual teacher Ram Dass. The phrase is also a simple yet profound instruction for life. I have shared these words with many clients as a mantra. One student I worked with found it so helpful, he had the phrase engraved on the inside of his university ring—to give him a *hand* staying present.

But what is presence?

When I do presentation training with clients, we inevitably talk about *stage presence*. This phrase means different things to different people, but I think of it as that elusive ability for someone to hold an audience in the palm of their hand. It's like the speaker is a magnet, someone the audience can't take their eyes off of. Many performers have bemoaned their deficit of this seemingly magical attribute, but how do you acquire stage presence? Are you born with it? Can you buy it? Manufacture it? There are certainly steps you can take to attempt to create stage presence, but that's attacking the challenge from the outside in, when it's really an inside job. Presence, whether onstage or off, is simply about being *present*.

I'd like to draw your attention to my use of language in the sentence above: "simply" is used to describe the definition, not the practice. Presence itself is both simple and one of the most complicated things to master. Like the Savasana pose at the end of a yoga class, it sounds easy but it is way more challenging than you might expect. This pose is also known as corpse pose, and involves lying on your back on the floor, and allowing your body and mind to come into stillness. Awake and aware, but still.

But wait...why is it so difficult to be present? Hmm, let's see, we live in a world that seems to spin faster every day. Our attention is fractured. I'm sure you've heard the oft-quoted statistic that we humans have an average of *seventy thousand* thoughts each day. I've heard many great teachers point to this as the reason we need a mindfulness practice. It's usually contextualized by the fact that the majority of those thoughts are the same ones we ruminated on yesterday and the day before, and the day before that. Think about it. Does this ring true for you? I definitely notice it in myself when I'm alert to my mind chatter.

The Surrender Experiment, a book by Michael (Mickey) A. Singer, is the riveting true-life story of what happens when you give in to the power of presence. The subtitle, *My Journey into Life's Perfection*, speaks volumes about what happened when the author discovered the magic of non-resistance. As a teenager, Singer struggled with anxiety and a frenetic mind, and at the age of twenty-two, a single moment changed everything. He found himself in an uncomfortable silence with a friend, and started actively noticing what he was thinking and how he was feeling. For the first time, he discovered he could observe his thoughts and emotions as they formed rather than just experiencing their fluctuation. This revelation evolved into a spiritual awakening which took Singer down a path to meditation, and an eventual decision to live life as an experiment: he would simply surrender to whatever twists and turns his path took. What unfolds is a fascinating story that includes both great peace and a multi-billion-dollar business.

It was this series of questions posed by Singer that spoke directly to me: "What if you woke up one morning and your arm was going up and down uncontrollably? You'd call someone, right?" He then asks, "Why don't we react the same way when it's our *mind* that's out of control?" He draws a comparison to a car, pointing out that while it's a tremendously useful and productive thing, it can also be dangerous if no one's at the wheel.

I use a car metaphor when I'm presentation coaching. If you live in a place that gets cold for part of the year, you probably know the feeling of driving on icy roads. There's a horrible sensation when you start to slide, and you realize you no longer have control of the vehicle. That is what it's like to go onstage when you're feeling anxious, and not present. In fact, I tell my clients that my main aim is not for them to pre*sent*, but to *pres*ent. Because that's the way to people's heads *and* hearts.

Part of the reason we find it magnetic to see someone who is truly present is because we wish we could achieve that state ourselves. Presence is equated with happiness because it signals that we are comfortable in our own skin, and therefore comfortable *letting others in*. A coveted sense of safety.

I heard another powerful description of presence recently, listening to the much-celebrated poet Ocean Vuong on an episode of the podcast *On Being*. He describes the tradition, in many Asian American homes, of removing one's shoes before entering. This, he explains, is an act of respect: "I'm going to take off my shoes to enter something important; I'm going to give you my best self." Vuong has taken that cultural belief and used it in his own "stage presence," when teaching: "I think, even consciously, when I read or give lectures or when I teach, I lower my voice; I want to make my words deliberate; I want to enter—I want to take off the shoes of my voice so that I can enter a place with care so that I can do the work that I need to do." What a beautiful act of being consciously present.

In my experience, though, presence requires *practice*. I understand that verb may have negative connotations for you. Trust me, it conjures up dreaded memories for me—and likely for my mother too, having to remind me incessantly as a kid to practice the piano. At the time, I would've definitely used the word "nagging" to describe her persistence, but now that I'm a mother of three myself, I have a softer perspective.

Here's what you need to remember, first and foremost: *Practice makes imperfect.* This is not about perfection! I'm totally imperfect—always slipping—but the difference is, now I catch myself. And that's the gift of presence. *I'm perfect.* Just drop the apostrophe and you've got *imperfect*. If only it were that simple for a perfectionist to get comfortable with imperfection. I'm here to tell you it *is* possible, but it takes practice to foster the readiness and willingness to drop your mask of perfection and Show UP.

As I often console myself, I'm no Buddhist master. I'm more practice than I am presence.

When my practice is haphazard, the way I show up in the world is haphazard. But even once I realized how necessary the practice of presence was, it took me a long time to incorporate it into my oh-so-busy life. How's this for a paradox? I crave presence, but I also seem to do everything in my power to avoid it. Unless it's a regular practice, my natural tendency is to allow fear to rule the roost—convincing me there's too many other things to do. And the more I lean into that busyness, the less time (and ability) I have for presence. The irony is that when I take time to be truly present, I'm no less efficient and effective—I'm *more*. More focused, more creative, and more alive.

Ultimately, being present is a gift you give to everyone around you, but primarily it's a gift to yourself. Can you step out of the stream of doing and thinking...to *feel* and *be*? Eventually, the goal is to develop the ability to stand in that stream and allow it to flow around you—without being swept away.

> *I know who I am*
> *   with my toes in the sand*
> *and the cool feel of stones in my hand*
>
> *as the waves travel in*
> *   and the waves travel out*
> *I let go of my fear and my doubt*
>
> *in this moment of stillness*
> *   my body exhales*
> *and my soul & my spirit take sail*
>
> *breathe in & breathe out*
> *   the ocean reminds me*
> *while the breeze whispers softly...*
> *   just be*

DOORWAYS TO PRESENCE

" Mindfulness" is a funny word. When you break it down, it suggests a practice of making the mind *full*, but my busy brain is my greatest challenge. I crave mind-emptiness. What I've discovered though, is that being *mindful* is very different than having a maxed-out mind. It's an antidote to a crammed cranium, and this incredible cure is easy, free, and available to everyone.

Mindfulness is the practice of being in the present moment, and its benefits have been well established and documented—not only by practitioners, but by scientists. It's been widely proven to help reduce stress levels, increase well-being, and improve concentration and focus. I've experienced all those benefits personally, but I've also found it an amazing tool for reducing my need for control, accepting what is, and shrinking my fear. Seeing myself and my life as a *sphere*.

The most well-known form of mindfulness is meditation, but I'm going to venture out on a limb here and say it's also the most dreaded. That's why I think any conversation about meditation should start with misconceptions. A look at what it's not instead of what it is.

I'm going to take you back to my metaphor of breath as a vehicle now, but I'm going to twist it just a bit. Most of us only use that vehicle for doing short errands. Meditation is like taking the vehicle of the breath on a great open highway. At first you only make it a few exits, but eventually, with practice, this vehicle can take you to places you've only dreamed of.

I remember how terrified I was as a sixteen-year-old when my drivers' ed course steered me out onto the highway for the first time. As I eased the car along the on-ramp, the instructor kept encouraging me to go faster. I was trying, but I was going against every instinct. Little teenage Gator GUS was squealing, "Nooooo! Too fast! Not safe! You can't do this! Pull over!" Fortunately, my common sense (and my enduring desire for gold stars) prioritized the teacher's voice over the silent shrieks of my fear. Putting my pedal to the metal, I gritted my teeth and resisted the strong temptation to close my eyes. I was going 80 kilometres an hour with cars whipping by like I was a horse and buggy, but I felt like I was hurtling through space, and I couldn't wait till it was over.

That's how I felt learning to meditate. Instead of moving fast, I had to sit still, in silence, and that was equally terrifying. Of course, there wasn't really anything silent about it. In fact, it was like giving GUS a megaphone. All I could hear was his constant reptilian chatter, all boiling down to: "You're a terrible meditator!"

Pema Chodron is a Buddhist nun, and the author of some incredibly helpful books, including *When Things Fall Apart* and *Don't Bite the Hook*. I found it so liberating the first time I heard her say that she had been meditating for decades and still hadn't managed to make her mind still. She has wonderful teachings on being compassionate with yourself as you learn to quiet the mind. Because of her, I learned to think of my active mind as a little child, and to be endlessly willing to catch my thoughts wandering and then gently guide them back to stillness.

That's the practice. Catch and release. Of the many things I've found to beat myself up about through the years, meditation was probably the most ironic. But in the same way that people shouldn't expect to be great public speakers without some training and practice, you shouldn't expect to master meditation in your first sitting—or in your first hundred! Maybe you've tried focusing on your breathing and found you were too busy chasing your monkey mind around the room to concentrate on your in-breath and out-breath. If so, don't listen to the voice that tells you you're not cut out for it. Maybe you just need a guide. Guided meditation has always worked best for me, and although a friend suggested years ago that this isn't 'real' meditation, I don't buy that. It was a great way *in* to the practice, and frankly it's still my favourite form.

There are many different types of meditation and also a variety of ways to learn. Go to a class, invest in an online course, surf YouTube for sessions, or go it alone. It's all about finding what's right for you. One easy option is to get into the "gap" between your thoughts, a user-friendly meditation method offered by Wayne Dyer. It involves simply focusing on your inhale and then hanging in nothingness for a few seconds before exhaling, and then hanging in that same nothingness before inhaling again. That "gap" between breaths is a gift that might surprise you.

But mindfulness is more than meditation, and in my experience there are easier ways to start than sitting on a mat wrestling with your mind. It's literally just about being relentlessly present. Here's a straightforward exercise that might help:

- Sit yourself down, settle into your space, and become a witness to what is around you by utilizing all your physical senses.
- See your surroundings, one aspect at a time. What do you notice when you really *look* intentionally at things?

- Let your eyes drift from one thing to another, lingering on each long enough to fully absorb it. Then close your eyes, eliminating the visual stimulation around you.
- What do you hear? Listen hard and simultaneously soften, allowing yourself to float in the auditory realm.
- Then tune into what you smell. Feel the air flowing in through your nostrils. What do you feel?
- Notice your heart beating. Then, take your attention to the big toe on your right foot. Can you feel the pulse of blood flowing through it? Then switch to your other toe.
- Now, feel your tongue. Be aware of the underside of it, how the tip of it rests against the back of your teeth. Is there a taste in your mouth? Is it moist or dry?

You don't have to engage in this practice for long to feel its calming effects, and the payoff is cumulative. Like exercising any other muscle, the more you do it, the better your results. And the good news is, you can practice it anywhere, any time. Whether you're sitting, eating, walking, driving, listening, knitting, painting, brushing your teeth, or washing the dishes, mindfulness is about devoting your attention to just that one activity without the interference of your thinking mind. It's about eliminating the default commentator or judge in your head.

Here's a down-to-earth example. Washing dishes has always been a chore for me, partly because my natural tendency when scrubbing pots and pans is to think—with resentment—about all the other things I could be doing with my time. Now, though, when I catch my mind taking over with complaints, I mindfully remember to feel the warm water on my hands, focus on my movement, and stay in the moment. I'm grateful to Eckhart Tolle for teaching me that routine activities present us with valuable opportunities to be completely present.

Perhaps my favourite mindfulness exercise is progressive relaxation; an exercise that reliably centres me. It's based on the idea that relaxing the muscles in our bodies helps to ease anxiety in our minds. Quite simply, it involves lying down and methodically tensing individual muscles for about five seconds, and then relaxing them, allowing all tension to melt away...and really noticing the difference.

This mind-body connection is the key to comfort—in my own skin, and in my life.

And now, I invite you to open a Doorway to Presence. These are practices that sustain and strengthen my own relationship with the present moment, and I return to them again and again. I offer them up humbly in the hopes they may serve you too!

SHOW YOUR LUNGS SOME LOVE

You know how, as we age, we tend to lose track of old friends? Sometimes you've just outgrown someone, or to put it in a kinder way, you've grown in different directions. But if you're like me, there are also friends from your past who you love, but life just got in the way. I'd like to ask you to consider something: is it possible this is a description of your relationship with your *lungs*? After all, when we were babies, we were fully acquainted with these miraculous air sacks with which we come equipped, and we made good use of them. Think about when you were a sleeping baby; your belly rising and falling with each full inhale and exhale.

Breath is life. But life is stressful, and anxiety and fear strangle our life force by impinging on our breath. Given all the technological advances we have access to, you would think we'd be living on easy street compared to our cave-dwelling ancestors, but it's not that simple. While the earliest humans experienced short-lived bouts of fight-or-flight during moments of danger, too many of us today live in that state all the time. When our breath gets shallow, our brains and our bodies suffer, and they let us know. To compound matters, most of us are walking around with a breath baseline that is already insufficient. Our lungs are woefully underemployed.

That's why James Nestor wrote what amounts to a user's manual for the lungs. His book *Breath, The New Science of a Lost Art* is a wakeup call for those of us who neglect to respect the role of respiration. In fact, Nestor wants to change the way the world breathes. But get this: he doesn't want us to breathe more; he wants us to breathe *less*. Here are two takeaways from this life-changing book: slow down your breathing, and stop breathing through the mouth. The evidence is compelling that both these bits of advice can make you healthier. Do yourself a favour and pick up his book, catch him on YouTube, or tune into his message on one of many podcasts.

———————

Breath is an incredibly effective tool to usher you into the present. In fact, just bringing your attention to your breath is calming. Don't take my word for it, though. Let's try a few exercises.

DEEP BELLY BREATHING

This exercise is aimed at recreating an infant's natural breathing pattern. It's easiest to master this while lying down, so first, get comfortable horizontally. Then rest one hand on your stomach and take your focus away from breathing into your chest. Instead, visualize a balloon in the cavity of your belly, and on each inhale, inflate the balloon so that your stomach rises and your ribs expand—to the front, sides, and back. Then let the breath go—not forcing it out, but simply allowing it to escape. Repeat. Take your time and pause briefly at the top and bottom of the breath (in the gap!).

This is a fantastic way to promote relaxation because it sends a message to your brain that you're not in danger and helps switch you from your sympathetic nervous system, which is geared toward protecting you (fight or flight) to your parasympathetic nervous system which is all about relaxation (rest and digest). Another way to achieve this is to breathe in for a count of four, stop breathing for a count of seven, and then exhale slowly to a count of eight. (Many people swear by this uneven count to help them fall asleep, so don't practice these breathing techniques while you're driving a car!)

Try starting with just a few repetitions and work your way up.

BOX BREATHING

If anxiety is an issue, box breathing is another great exercise.

Breathe in, fully inflating your lungs, for a slow count of five. Then, gently hold that breath for five seconds. (Try not to strain or clench.) Release the breath for another count of five, and then hold it again for five. Repeat.

ALTERNATE NOSTRIL BREATHING

This exercise is not only calming, but it's said to boost focus and stimulate creativity by encouraging a balance between the right and left hemispheres of your brain.

You can either use the index fingers of each hand, or you can hold one hand in front of your nose and take turns plugging your nostrils with your thumb and middle finger. I'll walk you through it using the right hand, but of course which hand you prefer to use is up to you.

- While holding your right nostril closed with your thumb, inhale through your left nostril.
- Then, with the right still plugged, plug the left nostril.
- Pause for just a second before you release your thumb on the right, and exhale through the right nostril.
- Inhale through that same right nostril, and then switch again, exhaling through the left.

So, the pattern is exhale, inhale, plug and switch, exhale, inhale, switch, exhale, inhale, plug and switch.

———

Give your lungs some license, and you might just be shocked by the power of oxygen to expand your life.

SING YOUR WAY TO VAGUS

Singing in the shower does more than get you clean; it's a great way to step squarely into the present moment. But would you believe it might also make you healthier by flipping a switch on your nervous system? You've heard the expression "What happens in Vegas, stays in Vegas." Well, the opposite is true for vagus. The longest cranial nerve, vagus is a super-connector between the brain and the body, facilitating vital communication between the heart, lungs, stomach, and brain. It's also capable of shifting gears from your sympathetic nervous system to your parasympathetic nervous system.

Recent research has shown that stimulating the vagus nerve shows promising results in lowering inflammation, helping to combat a number of illnesses—from rheumatoid arthritis to diabetes and cardiovascular disease. Because of its connection to your breathing, digestive function, and heart rate, stimulating the vagus nerve also has mental health benefits. According to the Mayo Clinic website, an implantable vagus nerve stimulator to treat epilepsy and depression is already FDA-approved.

But you don't need surgery to capitalize on the power of the vagus nerve to help you relax. There are a variety of ways to activate it, and thereby hack your system. My friend Rachel is a gifted massage therapist and energy healer, and she offers this easy exercise:

- Inhale deeply through the nose and slowly exhale with lips closed (humming) or allowing your mouth to open and your voice to make one long "haaaaaaaa" sound (toning).
- Repeat ten times.
- Bring your awareness to the vibration this creates in the head, neck, and torso.

Singing, humming, and chanting can all help trigger and tone the vagus nerve because it's connected to your vocal cords. I've always loved singing, but because I can't carry a tune in a bucket, my perfectionism silenced my voice for a long time. Now that I know it can improve my physical and mental health, I sing every day. I encourage you to try this practice on your own, or take it up an octave by harmonizing with others. If you've ever sung in a choir, you know the joy and sense of connection that springs from voices raised in unison. In fact, some of my favourite childhood memories are of singing around a fire at Camp Wapomeo. However if, in the spirit of that famous old Groucho Marx quote, you wouldn't want to belong to a choir that would have you as a member, consider an online option. One of my favourite artists, Coco Love Alcorn, runs a web-based community choir called the Wonderland Singers (*wonder landsingers.com*) that's open to everyone. Coco's got an infectious enthusiasm, a talent for teaching, and a supremely welcoming warmth. Or just put on your favourite playlist and sing along with abandon. Tune in and tone up your vagus nerve!

Other ways to engage this seemingly magical medicine include deep breathing, gargling, meditation, and cold therapy.

AN ICE IDEA

Please consult a physician before trying cold therapy.

In the interest of fully Showing UP, I need to tell you that I am a big baby when it comes to immersing myself in cold water. I love the beach, but even having lived most of my life on the east coast, I've been known not to grace the ocean with my bodily presence until late August when the temperature edges up to somewhere near 16 degrees Celsius (60°F). That would be like a hot tub for Wim Hof. The man who's become known the world over as "The Ice Man" has been polar plunging for almost fifty years. He's claimed many world records for prolonged exposure to ice (from swimming in frigid water to hanging out in enormous buckets of ice cubes), and he's climbed Mount Kilimanjaro wearing only a pair of shorts.

While I'm not prescribing this extreme approach for you (or me!), I believe we can learn something from Wim. Research shows his claims that cold therapy can radically improve your health to bear weight. Among the reported benefits touted on his website: reduced stress level, enhanced creativity, improved energy, better sleep, sharpened focus, better sports performance, and a stronger immune system. As I understand it, much of that is due to the fact that cold therapy lowers inflammation, which has proven to be the basis for many diseases and conditions, and Wim attributes this to cold therapy's stimulation of the vagus nerve.

I know several people who are devotees of the Wim Hoff Method (WHM) as it's helped them overcome depression and anxiety, and that's what really got my attention. But you don't need to cut a hole in the ice and take the plunge to bring yourself into the present moment.

Cold showers are an obvious entry point, and the good news is you can ease into this habit. I'm living proof. At the end of your normal shower, simply finish off with thirty seconds of cold water—as cold as you can stand it. It may not sound appealing, but once you've felt its energizing effects, you might discover the short-lived discomfort is worth it.

SHAKE IT UP, BABY NOW

If you saw my daily writing warm-up routine, you might be concerned for my well-being, but it's actually a vital part of my process: I spend five minutes in a full-bodied shake. Not because I'm nervous, but because it's a prescription that has proven positively priceless.

It's a practice espoused by Laraine Herring, the author of *The Writing Warrior: Discovering the Courage to Free Your True Voice*. The shaking is the second step in her three-part process (which also includes breathwork and freewriting), and although she uses it as a tool to teach writers, she originally learned it in Taoist yoga training. Its intention is to break up physical stagnation, open up channels of energy, and unlock creativity based in authenticity. But of course, you don't need to *write* to benefit from this simple practice.

Laraine's pitch reveals how shaking can be helpful to all of us:

Here's the best thing about [it]...You don't have to know what you want to work through. You don't have to create a framework for it to reveal its secrets to you. You just have to show up and shake and then observe yourself over the days and weeks that you're shaking.

I definitely practice shaking on days when I'm not writing, and my body and mind are better for it. It's actually aligned with advice I've received from a practitioner of Traditional Chinese medicine. He told me that just bouncing—while shifting weight from one foot to the other—or jogging in place for five minutes every day can radically improve overall health and wellness. I've since found that whether I bounce or shake, I notice a positive shift in my energy—or what the Chinese call the Qi (pronounced *Chee*)," or life force—and focus. In fact, I even have a Qi machine now—a contraption that sits on the end of my yoga mat and slides back and forth while cradling my ankles, shaking my body for me.

The book *Younger Next Year* by Chris Crowley and Henry S. Lodge presents a riveting case for perpetual motion. It's built on the foundational principle that our bodies are always either in a state of growth or decay. As the theory goes, when we slow down as we age, we're accepting decay. However, we can turn things around by *turning up* the intensity in our exercise routine. It presents a ton of evidence to support the idea that we can reverse the aging process by impacting the molecular makeup of our bodies. It's not easy—in fact it's a lot of work; hard workouts six days a week—but the payoff is worth it if, as they suggest, it enables people in the second half of their lives to "continue to live like fifty-year-olds until well into their eighties."

Depression is another compelling example of the connection between movement and mood. The science is crystal clear, with many studies proving that exercise can be as effective as an anti-depressant. According to the Mayo Clinic, "Doing 30 minutes or more of exercise a day for three to five days a week may significantly improve depression or anxiety symptoms." It also suggests that even doing as little as ten to fifteen minutes of exercise at a time "may make a difference." So how does it work? They answer that question with two main benefits: by "releasing feel-good endorphins and taking your mind off worries."

I think this is why runners tend to be so passionate about their chosen workout. It keeps them fit both physically and mentally! Don't despair if galloping's not your go-to. There are lots of other ways to get out of your head and into your body—from yoga, Pilates, and martial arts, to speed-walking, tennis, pickleball, swimming...or even dancing!

WHEN IN DOUBT, DANCE IT OUT

There are many challenges in relationships, and one of them is that both partners have to show up and be present. Great dance partners, like elite athletes, must be completely in the moment. For most of my life I was a bad dancer for this reason. You know the expression "Dance as if no one is watching"? I danced as if everyone was watching—and knew I was in more of a rut than a *groove!* I learned in grade nine when we did a dance unit in gym class that I had no aptitude for choreography. I know now this is part of my ADHD brain profile, but at the time it was just another reason to feel inadequate. The rest of the kids seemed to be able to get it—why couldn't I? I was focused on the mistakes I might make rather than being present for the learning. To hide my deficit, I did a two-step right into the role of class clown. It's the first time I remember being adept at making people laugh.

Decades later while on retreat at the Kripalu Institute, I learned about a daily lunchtime session called Noon Dance. Because of my lack of aptitude in this arena, I was reluctant to take part...until I discovered it was *my* kind of dance class. Picture a big room, lots of people, great music—and absolutely no rules. Every kind of movement is welcomed, and no one is watching you because they're all too busy being in the moment. Being in their own body. It's all about releasing restrictions and letting your inner child play. Of course, you can create your own free-form dance opportunity any time you want—in your kitchen, rec room, or even your backyard!

Turns out, dancing it out is also a great stress reliever. If you're familiar with the show *Grey's Anatomy*, this was Meredith and Christina's favourite way to let off steam, and I have become a convert. One day when I was experiencing my own frantic feelings before a live TV appearance, I was shocked by how noticeable my heartbeat was. I immediately saw this as an invitation to presence and started groovin' to the beat—of my heart. Talk about a pulsating dance. It worked like magic, and it's become my number-one solution for calming my nerves.

TAKE A BEAT

*"Music can change the world because
it can change people." –Bono*

I've always loved music, but it's only recently I've recognized its powerful emotional influence. The right song can swing my mood in the time it takes to traverse an octave. It's truly one of my most dynamic Doorways to Presence.

People say it soothes the savage beast, but that expression is a slightly twisted version of its origin. In his 1697 play, *The Mourning Bride*, William Congreve wrote: "Music has charms to sooth a savage Breast." It certainly soothes my heart when it's in overdrive, but it also has the power to *shift* me from one emotional state to another. Sad to happy, frustrated to elated, lazy to energized. It's an upper or a downer, whatever kind of fix you're looking for—in the healthiest way.

GO WITH THE FLOW

The ocean is a natural healer. I love and believe in the old saying (attributed to Isak Dinesen) that salt water is a cure for everything—whether it's tears, sweat, or the sea. There's something particularly special about being by the ocean—or a lake if you don't happen to have access to the edge of a continent! It may have something to do with the fact that our bodies are about 60 percent water. The ocean is also brimming with lessons about life. Here's a couple of examples of how I've found wisdom in water.

It's 2015 and I'm floating in the ocean off Kaanapali Beach, simultaneously experiencing relaxation and exhilaration. I'm watching with guilty amusement as fully grown adults venture into the seemingly calm ocean and get tumbled off their feet in the shallow water. I'm out beyond the break, allowing the current to move me, peaceful and content. Then the analogy hits me like a big wave washing over me: it is in the shallow waters of life that I lose my footing, constantly struggling for a sense of control, and consistently knocked off my equilibrium by a force greater than me. When I move into the deeper meaning of my life and cease my resistance to the "slings and arrows of outrageous fortune" (as Shakespeare so aptly put it), I can truly go with the flow.

Now, let's stay in the sea for a moment. There's another visual that's been a lifeline for me, but this one's much safer in the imagination: Picture yourself swimming in deep waters. The waves are choppy, and it's easy to get frantic—that's your fear taking over. Now, pause, and remember that all you have to do is allow yourself to sink to the bottom. On the ocean floor, it's calm, still, and magnificently peaceful. And since this is only an imaginary indulgence, you don't have to worry about sharks or a lack of oxygen. All you have to do is let yourself sink. Release, and let go. Somehow, imagining myself in a place without air brings me *back* to my breath. Back to myself. There is a deep sense of calm within you that you always have access to; it just takes practice to remember how to get there. Here's a simple mantra to remind you of this: *Sea Kelp* (if this doesn't make sense, say it loud until the humour bubbles to the surface!)

GET STONED

I truly believe that inspiration is everywhere, if only we're present enough to see and feel it. This particular exercise is proof positive; I discovered it while walking along the beach one day in my bare feet. I have a love affair with stones—well, I guess it might be unrequited love, but I do bring a lot of them home—and occasionally, my husband will humourously mutter, "Oh good, more rocks." But in my mind, there's a big difference between rocks and stones. I mean, c'mon. Stones have a soul.

When I was a child, my family would often drive along the South Shore of Nova Scotia—visiting friends or for a weekend getaway, and my mother would hit every antique joint on the route. It was like our station wagon was magnetically drawn to these shops, but the car was also packed to the gunnels with kids, all of whom would groan with each stop. I secretly didn't mind because I knew there was a chance I'd come away with a ten-cent polished stone. Diamonds might be some girls' best friends, but what can I say, I'm low-mainte-Nance!

Now, back to the beach and my sophisticated new meditation technique. I stooped to pick up an almost perfectly rounded stone the size of small cantaloupe. It was a beauty. And it felt calming just to hold it. It was heavy enough to hold down a tablecloth on a picnic table, but not too heavy to toss and catch. And that's just what I started to do. It immediately reminded me of the kettlebell exercise class I had taken a few years before—the way I would swing my arm from back to front and toss the stone gently into the air. It travelled up about a foot before gravity returned it to my palm. I absorbed it like a quarterback expertly pulling down a football. Steady and sure. Calm. Allowing the weight of it to swing my arm back down.

I knew immediately I was onto something good. Then I started to walk, while continuing the constant motion, and allowing it to become a full-bodied exercise: my right arm swinging up, releasing the stone, waiting, then receiving it with my left hand, and swinging that arm down and back up again. Like a pendulum with a bonus at one end. I continued till I reached the end of the beach, and I knew I had invented something meaningful. Eureka! This stone was unpolished; it was not a gem but it was a gift all the same. It was a ticket to the present.

You can do this anywhere. And if you can't get your hands on a stone, try a weighted ball, a full water bottle, or even a can of beans! Let me know if you love it.

LET YOURSELF OFF THE LEASH

There's nothing my dogs love more than a trip to the beach, and no wonder. There's a world of difference between a road walk on-leash, and the delicious liberation of running wild, bounding at will from the sand to the water. They are completely different experiences. But how often do you let *yourself* off the leash?

It occurred to me one day while watching my dogs play glee-fully that I rarely allow myself the same pleasure. Suddenly I chuckled, thinking about how the other humans on the beach might react if I were to start running as wildly as my pets—sniffing the long grass, then sprinting into the waves, only to pull a U-turn and throw myself into a soft dune, rolling energetically about till I was covered in sand. The irony is that although onlookers might question my sanity, this seemingly erratic practice might be good for my health—both physical and mental!

That's because play is a portal to presence. Some of the most memorable times from my childhood were vacations when we had family playtime. Rainbow Valley water park was our east coast version of Disney World, and whenever we made a summertime trek to Prince Edward Island, the excitement was palpable. I realize now it had a lot to do with my parents being *present* during those vacations. Like those old MasterCard ads, the entrance fee might've been five dollars, the candy corn might have been two dollars, but to witness adults at play...priceless.

Play = childlike wonder and curiosity = freedom.

As we leave childhood behind, play too often gets left behind as well. It's just for kids. Maybe we still indulge in sports or boardgames but all too often we adults choose play within a construct of competition where there are rules and expectations, a realm where our inner critic can still *thrive*.

My advice is to find your own field of dreams. A place where you can park your cellphone, sideline your self-judgement, and really meet the moment.

Letting yourself off the leash is about detaching yourself from the expectations of others and yourself. As one of my favourite poets on the planet, Mary Oliver, says in her beautiful poem "Wild Geese," "You do not have to be good..../You only have to let the soft animal of your body/love what it loves."

AFFIRM REMINDER

"Imagine if we obsessed about the things we love about ourselves."

I recently saw this anonymous quote and thought immediately of Louise Hay. That's exactly what she tried to encourage people to do to improve their self-love. She recommended a steady diet of affirmations; statements like "My self-esteem is high, because I honour who I am"; "I deserve the best, and I accept it now"; and "Life supports me in every possible way."

If you're like me, you've spent a lifetime unwittingly training your brain to think negative thoughts and giving your fear free rein. Affirmations are about gathering the reins back in your firm grasp and steering the horse of your mind in a more positive direction. So, why not try creating some of your own affirmations? My advice is to look at your perceived deficits and turn the tables. *Instead of beating yourself up, build yourself up.*

Some of my personal favourites are "Everything is working out"; "I am rooted in purpose and divinely supported"; and "I am love." Master Yap, the qigong teacher whose sequence I practice, ends his session with the following statements, which are powerful affirmations: "My blood and Qi are flowing smoothly. I am filled with peace and joy. I am free of pain and illness. I am blessed with good fortune."

If making these kinds of pronouncements seems ridiculous to you, consider the scientific argument for affirmations. You've probably heard of neuroplasticity, the firmly established concept that our brains are not static, but elastic. That they can stretch, grow, and adapt. Creating new neural pathways is like rewiring the brain—and guess what? A lot of studies have shown that affirmations have the potential to do just that! Learning a new language can enhance your brain, but an affirmative new vocabulary can also be positively uplifting.

ALTAR YOUR REALITY

Consider creating a space in your home that is dedicated to your practice of presence, and therefore, self-care. You can call it an altar, or if that conjures up too much religious connotation for you, call it an *alter*—a place that helps you alter your mindset. Let it be a space where you allow yourself peace—whether in the form of mediation, mindfulness, or even just listening to music. Once you've created a habit, muscle memory will kick in so that as soon as you sit down there (on a cushion or chair) your nervous system will shift gears.

You can populate your alter with items that inspire or calm you. On mine, I have a glowing salt lamp to represent my inner light, a laughing Buddha to remind me to not take life so seriously, beach stones to ground me, eagle feathers to represent the lift I get from being connected to Universal Presence, and a photo of me as a four-year-old (Fancy Nancy) to anchor myself in childlike joy and wonder.

What will *your* alter look like? Get creative, and have fun with it, gathering tokens and symbols that ground you and give you peace. Then give yourself time to just *be* in this space.

CHECK YOUR SELF

From the first promo clip of Apple TV's *The Morning Show*, I was hooked. It was bound to be up my alley—after all, it was about the behind-the-scenes workings of a TV newsmagazine, and to top it off, it starred two of my favourite actresses, Reese Witherspoon and Jennifer Aniston—the woman the world knows as "Jen." I've had a girl-crush on her for years, partly because she's so darned charismatic, but also because I could relate to her entrapment in a fishbowl—though her audience is infinitely bigger than mine ever was, and the crushing weight of scrutiny more than I can imagine.

In one powerful scene of the show, Aniston's character, Alex, finally shifts gears from Showing Off to Showing UP—on live TV. The script zeroes in on the injustice of Alex's whole life being in the public crosshairs simply because she chose to make her living on a screen, but no wonder the scene feels real. It's a breathtaking example of art imitating life, as this star steps out of her *persona* in favour of being the person she really is.

Consider this: a "screen" also refers to a tool used to filter out things we don't want—like dirt or insects or even viruses—and this seems an apt description of how I appeared on TV: filtered. I wasn't fully myself, but I was my self-*ish*; the self who was greedy for approval and attention. I was real-*ish*, authentic-*ish*.

So, here's a presence practice you can make a part of your daily life. Ask this question: are you showing the world your *self*, or your self-*ish*?

GET TO *WORK*

Suffering is optional. Remember that statement from the Dark section? It's a quote from the author and teacher Byron Katie, and I'm looping back to it now to share her powerful process called "The Work." It's a practice that involves actively questioning your own thoughts. You catch yourself in a stressful or painful thought, and then contemplate these four illuminating questions:

1. Is it true?
2. Can I know that it's true?
3. How do I react when I believe this thought?
4. Who would I be without this thought?

This exercise in presence and inquiry has helped millions of people around the world (and I'm one of them), but it started out helping Byron Katie. As she describes on her website, she was deep in darkness: "a ten-year-long downward spiral into depression, agoraphobia, self-loathing, and suicidal despair." When she hit rock-bottom, she had an awakening which led to a whole new outlook on life, and a personal and professional rebirth. If you're intrigued and want to know more about her story and her philosophy, I recommend her book *Loving What Is*.

I know "The Work" may sound ridiculously simple, but if you try putting it into practice, you may well find it *simply* profound.

PREPARE FOR YOUR WORST-CASE SCENARIO

When my younger sister was pregnant with her second child, she and her husband had an opportunity to take a special trip to Paris. To help facilitate this last adventure before the new baby, I travelled to Venice Beach, California, to stay with my nephew, who was a toddler at the time. It was my first visit to their home since they'd become parents, and I got a kick out of seeing all the baby locks on the kitchen cupboards. When I teased my sister that it was overkill to have plastic locks on the upper cupboards, she looked at me with a wry smile and said, "No, Nance, those are for earthquakes." It turns out if you live in SoCal, you don't want to clean up broken glass every time the earth shakes. *Gulp.* She then proceeded to show me where their "earthquake kit" was. It had everything they could need in the event of a bad quake. Did it make me feel better? Absolutely not. Just knowing that I might need it made *me* quake!

But I'll tell you when being prepared for a worst-case scenario *did* help me. I've talked about how consumed I was early in my TV career with making mistakes. And how I finally figured out that not only did mistakes not doom me to failure, but they could endear me to my audience—as long as I handled them with humour.

When you're hosting a live newsmagazine, there's a lot of moving pieces and a lot that can go wrong. In fact, it's the rare occasion when nothing goes wrong in a show. The trick is preventing the audience from seeing those glitches. However, there are times when you truly have no choice, and one day I realized I needed to create a safety net—a personal emergency-preparedness kit—for myself. For the potential of all hell breaking loose. Like it often did in my stressful TV dreams: it's the middle of the show and there's no script, the teleprompter dies, and the director's off on a coffee break.

Getting hung out to dry is no show host's idea of a good time. But it can happen. So instead of letting the fear hover over me like a permanent rain cloud, I came up with a "bit" that I could turn to if everything fell apart. It involved giving the viewer a glimpse behind the curtain and being authentic about what was happening—and thereby making it just another type of entertainment:

Okay folks, here's the thing about TV news. When things go smoothly with our production, what we do looks effortless. But the truth is, there's a lot of moving pieces that have to fit together to keep that veneer intact, and right now we're having some technical difficulties. Instead of being stressed out, and trying to pretend everything's okay, I'm going to make lemonade out of these lemons, and give you a little behind-the-scenes tour!

Knowing I had that response in my "back pocket" was transformative for me, and I highly recommend this tactic when you're faced with any anxiety-provoking circumstance. If you're prepared for the worst, you can make the *best* of a bad situation.

EXPRESS YOUR SELF

The author Joan Didion famously said, "I don't know what I think until I write it down," and that has often proven true in my life. I believe that's the foundational idea behind "Morning Pages," a practice prescribed by *The Artist's Way: A Spiritual Path to Higher Creativity*, a book by Julia Cameron. As the subtitle suggests, this book is more than a creativity guide. You could call it a program or a course, but I think of it as a way of life focused on helping people discover and recover their creative selves by breaking through their self-constructed blocks. Here's its central premise: all too often, when we set the intention to create, we end up creating roadblocks to our own production.

Cameron's words have resonated deeply for me. Here's a case in point: "I have learned as a rule of thumb, never to ask whether you can do something. Say instead, that you are doing it. Then fasten your seat belt. The most remarkable things follow." Her book suggests that everyone is creative, and that this outlet can offer a world of self-expression and exploration—but to create, we need to get past our fear. *Preach it, sister!*

Similarly, Brené Brown talks about "art scars," caused by shaming events in childhood, that make us pack up our creativity for life. I was well into adulthood when I realized this truth. I had adored art as a kid, but Comparison & Judgement (c&j) had caused me to leave it behind. As the daughter of a talented portrait artist, my best friend's creativity got a lot of attention. She even had beautiful handwriting, and people were forever commenting on how artistic she was. So, I made the inference that I was not. And that was that...until I was in my thirties, and out of nowhere, I developed a burning desire to paint again.

What I've discovered since is that art is an exceptional pathway to presence. Whether you're drawing, painting, writing, sculpting, knitting, sewing, woodworking, even putting together a puzzle—these activities require hyper focus, and because of that, they bring you into the present moment. I encourage you to discover this for yourself. Just beware of those fear-based blocks, which often appear in the form of what I call "status stackers." It's not about how your creation measures up to anything else, and it really doesn't matter *what the neighbours think*!

My poems are a case in point. Whenever I share them, I'm quick to issue a disclaimer that I recognize they're primitive, but that's a bad habit from an old paradigm. They are simple, yet meaningful to me, and writing them brings me peace and pleasure. And whenever I have the guts to share them publicly, they resonate with others. My friend Seàn is an Irish expat and a professor of English with an astounding ability to awaken an appreciation of poetry in others. Despite his sophisticated understanding of the art form, he's been encouraging of my own simple attempts. One day, he made this statement about our human inclination toward self-criticism: "We want our initial creativity to measure up to the work of masters." This is why a blank canvas is terrifying for so many of us, but it's also a potent reminder to come back to the practice of presence.

Morning Pages are a blank canvas every day. Here's the concept: sit down and write. Don't think, just write. Allow the words to pour onto your page as soon as they drift into your mind. No editing, no second-guessing, and no judgement. You'll likely find what lands on the page surprising, intriguing, or maybe even instructive.

Even if you think you have no artistic talent whatsoever, try sidelining your fear to indulge the creative child within. You might just end up painting your pain, singing your blues, or writing your wrongs.

RING YOUR OWN BELL

In the classic film *It's a Wonderful Life*, little Zuzu memorably tells her father, "Every time a bell rings, an angel gets its wings." Of course, Clarence is the angel in that movie and he ends up saving George's life by reconnecting him to his own Light. For me, watching it every December is not just entertaining, it's grounding...because the concept of recognizing our own value to the world is inspiring and comforting all at once. But I've also made a practice of incorporating Zuzu's bell notion into my daily life.

Imagine this. You're in the middle of a busy day, juggling more tasks than you'd like, feeling flustered by life. Then, your phone rings. How do you feel in that instant? Faced with this situation, I used to often feel like that ring pushed me over the edge—into the abyss of overwhelm. But then, a simple idea changed my life. Ten years ago, a yoga teacher suggested making one small change that she promised could have a huge impact on my stress level. It worked wonders for me, so now I'm sharing it with you.

Every time the phone rings, make it a reminder to *breathe*. Instead of rushing to pick up, let the ring bring you into the present moment. Take a deep breath. If you're visually oriented, build on this by picturing yourself actually flipping a switch marked RESET. Feel the difference in your body and mind...and *then* answer the phone!

STAY TUNED

When I started *The Soul Booth* podcast, I wanted to come up with a catchy sign-off, so I began brainstorming. When "Stay tuned!" dropped into my head, I literally squealed with delight. It was a nod to my past career in television, and a parting salutation that would encourage people to come back for more. But its *real* meaning was vibrational.

Long ago, Albert Einstein said, "Everything in life is vibration" and if you remember your high school chemistry class, you know what he was talking about; that all matter is made of atoms which are in a constant state of motion. Things that appear solid, aren't, and our bodies and minds are actually sophisticated energy conductors.

As I see it, when we are in *tune* with Universal Presence, we're in a positive vibration, but when we're cranky and overwhelmed, we're off-key. Human beings are instruments that require regular tuning. We all know how sweet it feels to be hitting the right notes, and to be working in harmony with others. The secret is finding what helps keep you tuned—whether it's music, exercise, time in nature, meditation, or a habitual gratitude practice—and then giving yourself that gift.

In a way, it's about being tuned in to yourself. Tuned in to your gut instincts and intuition. And tuned in to the frequency of love. My genuine wish is that these Doorways to Presence have in some small way helped you find a *good vibration*.

TO BE CONTINUED

This is where the end of the book should be. But here's the thing: there is no end to this book. The practice is *to be continued*. I hope I've conveyed this fundamental message: I am not someone who has it all figured out. As I said in my introduction, writing this book provided me with a whole lot of opportunity to practice presence. To shake off my inner impostor. But I'm clearly still in the struggle. The juicy, challenging, enlivening, frustrating, delightful struggle. More than anything, though, I am so damn grateful—for everything I've learned, for all the amazing opportunities I've had, and most of all for the people in my life. As Ted Lasso said, I feel like I "fell out of the lucky tree and hit every branch on the way down, and ended up in a pool of cash and Sour Patch Kids."

That gratitude extends to the many people who have supported me in becoming an author. Terrilee Bulger at Nimbus took a leap of faith and changed my life—by first agreeing to be my publisher, and then by giving me the perfect editor. Whitney Moran hopped on board wholeheartedly and helped in a more significant way than I can put into words. She served as teacher, coach, and confidante, and Showed UP every step of the way. I was also blown away by the way in which my husband, children, family, and dear friends embraced this new adventure, and fortified me with their love and support. And then there's you. I'm deeply appreciative of your willingness to come along on this journey, so I'm committing to *continue* sharing Doorways to Presence. Visit nancyregan.ca and subscribe to my newsletter if you want in on the action. And by the way, this is a two-way street. Remember, we're all each other's teachers *and* each other's students, so I want to hear from you. What are *your* favourite Doorways?

I'll sign off with this three-pronged wish that is my own special mantra: *Find joy. Stay safe. Be love.* And of course, a poem.

> *serenity*
> *isn't easy*
> *sometimes it flows*
> *through tears*
> *it's pursued through hours*
> *of arduous work*
> *that quickly turn to years*
>
> *when I feel like a broken record*
> *I remember I don't need to be fixed*
> *the spiral serves up lots of joy*
> *but also—its share of tricks*
>
> *it fools me into complacency*
> *—believing it's all figured out*
> *then loops me back to the start*
> *where I'm mired in fear and doubt*
>
> *like the Universe that's within me*
> *there are patterns along with the pain*
> *with presence & practice I see them*
> *and set off on my path again*